WAR-TIME JEWS:
THE CASE OF ATHENS

Alexander Kitroeff

WAR-TIME JEWS:
THE CASE OF ATHENS

Alexander Kitroeff

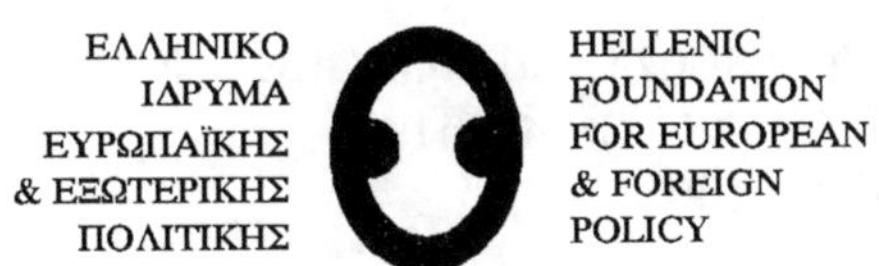

This publication was made possible thanks to the kind support of the Central Board of Jewish Communities in Greece and the Solon Allalouf family.

WAR-TIME JEWS: THE CASE OF ATHENS

Alexander Kitroeff

Copy editor: Youla Goulimis
Cover page: Marianna Veremis
Desktop publishing: Yannis Mandalidis, Anna Soulantika
Assistants: Pindaros Charissiadis, Georgios Kefalas, Natassa
Papacosta, Androniki Tzivanaki, Nicholas Yatromanolakis

HELLENIC FOUNDATION
FOR EUROPEAN AND FOREIGN POLICY
ELIAMEP
Akadimias 17, GR-10671, Athens, GREECE
Tel.: (+301) 36 37 627, 36 41 519
Fax: (+301) 36 42 139

Contents

PREFACE

Among the many unspeakable horrors that brought the near total destruction of Greek Jewry by the Nazis during World War II there lies a paradox: on the one hand, few countries in Europe lost a higher proportion of their Jewish population, yet on the other hand, the non-Jewish population in Greece can be credited with valiant efforts to save their Jewish compatriots. The texts that follow are intended to shed some light on those efforts and to place them in a broader national and Balkan perspective. While calling the reader's attention to the initiatives taken by several organizations and individuals to try and save the Greek Jews from being destroyed by the Nazis, these texts cannot be read without acknowledging the awful truth, namely that only 10,000 out of a total of between 70,000 and 80,000 thousand Jews did not perish in the Holocaust. It is all those deaths that we should remember first, before looking beyond and recording the heroic deeds of those who risked their lives in order to mitigate the human catastrophe that was unfolding in wartime Greece. A great deal of research has been undertaken on the Holocaust and on its impact in Greece since these texts were originally published but they remain relevant, if only as a reminder of the particular circumstances under which some help was offered to the

Jews of Greece. To focus on certain particular cases, as that of Athens is not to suggest that the Jews of Greece were uniformly aided by their fellow Greeks in their hour of distress. The purpose of highlighting those instances when the Nazi plans to destroy Greek Jewry were confounded, obstructed and stymied, is to show that prejudice and fear can be overcome by political commitment and individual initiative. Those initiatives taken in aid of the Greek Jews were heroic acts of resistance that often went against the grain of religious or cultural prejudice that pierced the social separation between Greek Gentile and Jew, especially in the case of Thessaloniki and the lands that had been incorporated into Greece only three decades earlier. With so many Greek Jews having perished during World War II those acts provide a limited sense of moral satisfaction, but they are, nevertheless, a shining moment in modern Greek history.

This publication was made possible thanks to the initiative of the Hellenic Foundation for European and Foreign Policy (ELIAMEP) and the financial support of the Central Board of Jewish Communities in Greece. I am also grateful to Francine, Daisy and Joseph Allalouf for their generous support — in memory of Solon Allalouf, decorated officer in the Hellenic Army during World War II.

New York University,
The A. S. Onassis Center
for Hellenic Studies,
November 1995

APPROACHES TO THE STUDY
OF THE HOLOCAUST IN THE BALKANS

Approximately one million of the eight million Jews that inhabited pre-World War II Europe lived in the Balkan Peninsula countries. Yet Balkan Jewry as a whole and each of the Jewish communities in the separate Balkan countries have not been accorded the place they deserve in Jewish historiography and in the study of the Holocaust.

This chapter begins with a description of the prewar status of Balkan Jews and of primary studies on Jewish life in the Balkan countries prior to World War II. Following the introductory section, the main part of the chapter reviews both the Jewish experience in each of the Balkan countries during the war and the principal studies relating to the Holocaust in those countries published in important works in Hebrew.[1] Also, the main themes and debates among scholars studying the wartime fate of the Jews in the Balkan countries are identified and analyzed. The chapter concludes by locating the work on wartime Balkan Jewry within more general trends in Holocaust historiography.

The Jews in the Prewar Balkans

The Jewish population in each of the Balkan countries has failed to attract the scholarly attention that Jewish communities elsewhere in Europe have. This can be explained in part by their relatively small size. Indeed, the only Jewish community in the Balkans that has been studied with any degree of thoroughness the Romanian, which was the third largest in prewar Europe. Other explanations for this apparent oversight include the generally peripheral status of the Balkan countries in mainstream European historiography and the contrasts between the principally Sephardic traditions of Balkan Jewry and the Ashkenazic traditions of most of European Jewry.

Little scholarly attention has been paid, moreover, to the study of Jews of the Balkans as a whole. It is true that following the post-World War II establishment of Communist regimes in Albania, Bulgaria, Romania, and Yugoslavia, most Western scholars ceased to regard the Balkans as a common region. The period during and preceding that war, however, was one in which several similarities obtained among the countries of the Balkan Peninsula. These similarities were expressed through the shared political traditions of the Balkan states, the characteristics of the dominant religion in the area, Eastern (Greek) Orthodox, and finally, the common traditions of the Jewish communities in these countries.

The status of minorities in the Balkan countries in the first half of the twentieth century was strongly influenced by the shared Ottoman past of these countries. The Ottoman Empire's system of government was one that tolerated multiethnic cohabitation. The Ottoman policy of allowing non-Islamic minorities a degree of autonomy, alongside the protection offered to minorities by the European powers, helped to preserve the various ethnic cultures

That ethnic mosaic shattered, however, with the advent of European nationalism in the nineteenth century and its diffusion among the Balkan bourgeoisie and intelligentsia.[2] The subject peoples of the Ottoman Empire (and those in the Balkan territories ruled by the Austro-Hungarian Empire) did not embrace nationalism simultaneously; the more economically powerful and better educated groups were its earliest adherents. While these groups eventually succeeded in forming independent nation-states, the other less economically and politically advanced ethnic groups lagged behind. When they did eventually embrace nationalist doctrines, they found that they were already incorporated into a national entity. Their challenges to the nation that had incorporated them resulted in continual unrest and friction over disputed boundaries and territories, with one nation often adopting the cause of a minority group of a neighboring country. Indeed at times, fierce intra-Balkan territorial disputes brought along the involvement of rival European powers, earning the Balkans the name "powder keg of Europe".[3]

The end of World War I brought about the final dissolution of the Ottoman and Austro-Hungarian empires and the more or less permanent settlement of the boundaries dividing Balkan national states. Several ethnic, linguistic, and religious groups found themselves incorporated into one or more of the six Balkan states, Albania, Bulgaria, Greece, Romania, Turkey, and Yugoslavia. At the same historical juncture, the newly formed League of Nations decided to guarantee the rights of national minorities in its member countries. The observance of minority rights by states was thus made a condition of admission to membership in the League of Nations. Those rights were guaranteed by the so-called minority treaties signed between the Allied powers and Greece, Romania, and the Kingdom of Serbs, Croats, and Slovenes (which was renamed Yugoslavia in 1929), and in special provisions in the peace treaties that the Allied powers signed with Bulgaria and Turkey.

The provisions in both these treaties can be divided between those that protected a minority's common rights (what would today be described as human rights) and those designed to preserve the identity of minority populations. Common rights included the acquisition of nationality based on habitual residence or birth in the national territory of one's parents; the protection of life and liberty; the free exercise in public or private of any creed, religion, or belief; and equal access to employment opportunities. Identity rights included the right of minorities to establish charitable, religious, and social institutions and schools as well as the right to free use and instruction of language.[4]

In the light of still-lingering nationalist and territorial rivalries, the Balkan states were sensitive to the possibility of a minority group within their borders playing the role of a "fifth column", acting in the interests of a neighbouring country. Several minorities, therefore, occasionally faced difficulties in the use and instruction of their respective languages. But due in part to their past Ottoman experience, the Balkan states remained tolerant on matters of religious freedom. Some states had a poorer record than others in minority policies. On the whole, the policies of Bulgaria, Greece, and Yugoslavia were only mildly hostile to certain minority groups. By contrast, Romania, Turkey, and to a lesser extent Albania all reserved far harsher treatment for minority groups within their borders.

The Jews were a significant minority group in all Balkan states. The Jewish communities in the Balkan countries consisted primarily of Sephardic Jews who had been welcomed by the Ottomans after their expulsion from the Iberian Peninsula in the late fifteenth century. The large number of Sephardic Jews-over twenty thousand settled in the city of Salonika alone-joined much smaller indigenous and assimilated "Romaniot" Jewish communities. As a consequence of the Ottoman system of government that granted a degree of self-autonomy to non-Islamic religious minorities, the Sephardic communities remained self-contained and unassimilated. A greater degree of assimilation was achieved by the Ashkenazic Jews who moved from Poland and Russia to the northern Balkan regions in the nineteenth century.

The largest Jewish community in the prewar Balkans was the Romanian, amounting to about 756,930 according to the Romanian census of 1930 and comprising 4.2 percent of the population. The Jewish community in Greece numbered 79,950, equivalent to 1 percent of the population, while the Yugoslav Jewish population of 71,342 accounted for 4 percent of the population, and the roughly 50,000 Jews in Bulgaria comprised slightly under 1 percent of that country's population.

While the population of all four of these countries was primarily rural, the Jews formed an almost exclusively urban element engaged in retail trade, commerce, and handicrafts. During the interwar period the largest Jewish urban concentration was in Thessaloniki (formerly Salonika until it was incorporated into Greece in 1912), where the community made up 20 percent of the city's population. The second-largest urban concentration of Jews was in the Bulgarian capital of Sofia, where over one half of the Jewish population of the country settled. The Jews in Yugoslavia lived, for the most part, in the cities of Belgrade, Sarajevo, and Zagreb. Romania was the only exception to this pattern, its Jewish populations having settled in several cities, towns, and even villages.

The Jews were among the least politically threatening ethnic groups. Other minorities, such as Armenians and Kurds had entertained notions of national self-determination at the territorial expense of the countries they inhabited.

The Balkan Jews, however, were much less nationalistically oriented. Sephardic Jews, who comprised the majority in Albania, Bulgaria, Greece, and Turkey and about one half of the total Jewish presence in Romania and Yugoslavia, were not particularly attracted to Zionism. Only the Bulgarian Jewry could boast of a committed Zionist movement. The indifference of most of the Sephardic and Ladino-speaking Balkan Jews toward Zionism can be explained by the primarily Ashkenazic and Yiddish-language characteristics of the early Zionist movement. Also, the Sephardic Jewry's experience with autonomy in the multiethnic Ottoman Empire strongly influenced its preference for maintaining its identity through a religious, rather than a nationalistic, consciousness.

The Jews in Bulgaria, Greece, Turkey, and Yugoslavia enjoyed the civic rights and political equality formalized in the post-War I minority treaties. Although Jewish religious freedom was also generally respected, some obstacles were occasionally placed in the way of the use and instruction of their language. Anti-Semitism was practiced only by small, peripheral pro-Nazi groups that would become more powerful in the late 1930s.

Romania was the only Balkan country in which the state pursued anti-Semitic policies, failing to respect the minority treaty it signed and refusing to extend Romanian nationality to all Jews living in its territory. In fact, anti-Semitism manifested itself in Romania as early as the second half of the nineteenth century, its intensity paralleling the anti-Semitism that took hold across the border in imperial Russia.

What lay at the root of Romanian anti-Semitism is a matter of debate, but if one takes into account the situation in the rest of the Balkans, one can exclude political causes. Despite the intensity of nationalist rivalries in the region, the Jews did not figure prominently as objects of nationalist hostility. Moreover, religiously based anti-Semitism cannot be considered as a prime motivating force. The Eastern (Greek) Orthodox church, for instance, less concerned with doctrinal definitions than the Catholic church, preferred to ignore the relatively tiny number of non-Greek Orthodox in Southeastern Europe. But as in other aspects of the history of this region, generalizations are risky and, in stark contrast to the attitude of the church elsewhere in the Balkans, the Romanian church did condone anti-Semitic behavior.

Nonetheless, the principal causes of Romanian anti-Semitism were probably economic. Romania distinguished itself from the other Balkan countries on the issue of land tenure. The local landowning group, the boyars, was powerful enough to frustrate the attempted land reform of 1864. The Romanian peasantry thus remained subjected to a harsh quasi-feudal state of affairs, by far the worst situation experienced by peasants in the entire Balkan region. The Romanian state, however, found it more convenient to blame the peasantry's hardships on the "misdeeds" of middleman minorities in towns and villages — Jews and to a lesser extent Greeks and Armenians, many of whom had become land leaseholders through moneylending — rather than on the boyars. That strategy was successful, as evidenced by an abortive 1907 peasant revolt directed against Romanian landlords and Jewish leaseholders.

In the 1930s most European countries witnessed the rise of fascism and authoritarianism. The Balkan countries were no exception, and by the second half of the 1930s Bulgaria, Greece, Romania and Yugoslavia were all ruled by authoritarian dictatorships. These regimes were more akin to Italian fascism than German Nazism, and they did not therefore pursue explicitly anti-Semitic policies. Moreover, the ethnic heterogeneity of the populations of the Balkan countries mitigated against the spread of Nazi theories of racial superiority that, in turn, would have contributed to the spread of anti-Semitism.[5]

The history of the Jews in the Balkans in the period preceding World War II is dealt with in the following works. The life of Jews in the Ottoman Empire is described in Abraham Galante, *Documents officiels Turcs concernant les juifs de Turquie* (Official Turkish documents concerning the Jews of Turkey), and Bernard Lewis, *The Jews of Islam*. Sephardic life is depicted in Michael Molho, *Usos y costumbres de los Sefardies de Salonica* (Habits and customs of the Sephardics in Salonica). There are no detailed studies examining prewar Balkan Jewry as a single group, only a short article that introduces such an angle by Daniel J. Elazar, "The Sunset of Balkan Jewry", *Forum 27*, no. 2 (1977): 135-41.

The main studies on the Bulgarian Jews in this

period are somewhat dated. They include A. Romano, Joseph Ben, and Nisim (Buko) Levy, *Yehudut Bulgariyah* (The Jews of Bulgaria), a general history of the Bulgarian Jews from earliest times; Saul Mezan, *Les Juifs espagnols en Bulgarie* (The Spanish Jews in Bulgaria); and N. M. Gelber, "Jewish Life in Bulgaria", *Jewish Social Studies* 8 (1946): 103-26.

The standard works on the Jews of Greece are by Joseph Nehama, *Histoire des Israelites de Salonique* (History of the Jews of Salonica), and I. S. Emmanuel, *Histoire des Israelites de Salonique* (History of the Jews of Salonica). See also Leon Sciaky, *Farewell to Salonica*. For the early twentieth century, a useful article is by Rena Molho, "Venizelos and the Jewish Community of Salonika, 1912-1919". A study of Greek interwar politics by George Th. Mavrogordatos, *Stillborn Republic: Social Coalitions and Party Strategies in Greece, 1922-1936*, provides an insightful analysis of the relations between the state, the political parties, and the Jewish community in Thessaloniki.

For prewar Romania, Oskar I. Janowsky, *People at Bay: The Jewish Problem in East Central Europe*, is an early, yet extremely useful analysis of the economic roots of anti-Semitism. Ezra Mendelsohn, *The Jews of East Central Europe between the World Wars*, offers an excellent account of the history of the Jews in the interwar period. This is one of the most important recent contributions to the immediate historical background to the Holocaust. The chapter on Romania describes the divisions between the assimilationist Jews of "Old" (Regat) Romania and the Zionism of the Jews in the Romanian territories to the west and north. The policies of the Romanian state toward the Jews in this period are sensitively analysed.

The Jewish community of interwar Yugoslavia is the only one in the Balkans to have been the subject of a book-length study based on extensive archival research. Harriet Pass Freidenreich, *The Jews of Yugoslavia: A Quest for Community,* focuses on the country's three communities, in Belgrade, Sarajevo, and Zagreb, and analyzes the socio-economic background of the communities, communal affairs, and issues of identity. This is by far the most thorough treatment of any of the Jewish communities in the Balkans during this period.

Finally, there are no studies on the Jews in interwar Albania and Turkey. Some information about the Jews in interwar Turkey can be gleaned from encyclopedias of Judaism and the *American Jewish Yearbook.* Neither community, however, was directly involved in the Holocaust.

The Holocaust in the Balkans

The fortunes of the Balkan countries during World War II were mixed. Greece and Yugoslavia fought against the Axis but were eventually occupied by German, Italian and Bulgarian forces. Bulgaria and Romania sided with the Axis powers, and Romania allowed German troops to be stationed in its territory. Hitler rewarded the two collaborationist Balkan countries by allowing their troops to occupy territories that

Bulgaria and Romania had either lost when the war broke out or that had formerly belonged to neighboring states. Thus Romania took over Bessarabia and Northern Bukovina, both of which had been lost to the Soviet Union, but did not recover Northern Transylvania, which the Nazis awarded to Hungary. Bulgaria occupied Western Thrace, which had formerly belonged to Greece, the Macedonian province of Yugoslavia, and the area known as Dobruja, which had belonged to Romania.

In the aftermath of their occupation of the Balkans, the Nazis did not move simultaneously against Jewish communities in each of the countries. They began rounding up Jews in occupied Yugoslavia in 1942 and Jews in occupied Greece more than a year later. The heavy-handed military control the Nazis exercised in both these countries facilitated widespread arrests of Jews, despite several efforts by the non-Jewish population to protect the community. Indeed, the rounding up of Jews in Greece was complicated by the growth of a powerful local resistance movement that successfully protected several Jewish communities. The German presence in Bulgaria and Romania was not strong enough to permit the rounding up and deportation of the Jews. Moreover, the pro-Axis status of both countries made it incumbent upon Berlin to seek the prior consent, as well as the assistance, of the Bulgarian and Romanian governments. In what must surely be one of the paradoxes in Balkan wartime history, both these governments resisted Nazi pressure to deport Jews. Yet the Bulgarian and Romanian governments did themselves oversee the rounding up and deportation of Jewish communities in the peripheries of their enlarged states — Bessarabia, Northern Bucovina, Yugoslav Macedonia, and Western Thrace. In fact, the roundups by the Romanians were particularly brutal and contrasted sharply with the Romanian government's refusal to arrest the Jews in the territories in the core of Romania, known as "Old" (Regat) Romania.

There are no studies that systematically examine the unfolding of the Holocaust in the entire Balkan region. Instead, the standard works on the Holocaust in Europe normally include separate accounts of the fate of the Jews in each of the Balkan countries, and these will be examined in the following section. These accounts rely heavily on monographs that focus on the situation of the Jews in each of the Balkan countries. The issues that are addressed in each cluster of country-based monographs are those that have been central to Holocaust studies elsewhere in Europe. The earliest works were "martyrological" in nature, seeking to highlight the fate of the Jews during the war. As work on the Holocaust in Western and Eastern Europe gradually developed into new areas of inquiry such as Gentile-Jewish relations, the "passivity" of the Jews, the responsibilities of the Jewish communal leadership, the role played by pro-Nazi governments, and the response of anti-Fascist resistance movements, the church, and ordinary people, studies on the Jews in the wartime Balkans also began exploring these areas. The specific conditions that prevailed in each of the Balkan countries have determined the relative stress that scholars have placed on each of these issues.

Bulgaria

The pro-Nazi government in Bulgaria implemented a series of anti-Semitic measures early on, but refused to comply with Nazi demands to deport the Jews. The head of state, King Boris, and members of the Sobranie (parliament) participated in the decision to resist Nazi pressure. Astonishingly, there were more Jews in Bulgaria at the end of the war than there had been when the war broke out.

A great deal of the work published on the situation of the Bulgarian Jews adopts a polemical tone in assessing the role played by the king and other officials. Nonetheless, in an effort to draw attention to the fact that there was little anti-Semitism among the population and that the small Communist resistance opposed the deportations, some other authors have chosen to stress the protection afforded the Jews by ordinary people and by the resistance movement.

The standard work in this field is Frederick B. Chary's *The Bulgarian Jews and the Final Solution, 1940-1944,* a thoroughly researched study that examines events in Bulgaria within the overall political context of the period. Chary's comprehensive study concludes that in themselves, the roles played by the king, the Sobranie, and the resistance movement were all ultimately minimal and that Jews were in fact protected only because the Bulgarian elite felt ambivalent and Nazi pressure was applied too late to be effective.

A compromise was reached, with the Bulgarians agreeing to the deportation of the Jews in the Yugoslav and Greek territories they had occupied and the Nazis allowing the Jews of Bulgaria to be sent to that country's provinces rather than face deportation. Interestingly enough, Chary concurs with a majority of studies on Bulgaria in finding that neither the church nor the general population was anti-Semitic, a conclusion that also tallies with what has been found for neighboring Greece and Yugoslavia. Also very useful are shorter scholarly treatments of these issues: a chapter in Marshall L. Miller's *Bulgaria During the Second World War*, pages 93-106, which provides a comprehensive summary based on documentary evidence, and an article by Nissan Oren, "The Bulgarian Exception: A Reassessment of the Salvation of the Jewish Community", *Yad Vashem Studies on the European Jewish Catastrophe and Resistance* 13 (1969): 83-106. See also Frederic Chary's "The Bulgarian Writers' Protest of October 1940 Against the Introduction of Antisemitic Legislation into the Kingdom of Bulgaria", *East European Quarterly* 4 (March 1, 1970): 88-93.

Among the previously mentioned "polemical" works, which do, however, provide valuable information, are the following. Benjamin Arditi, *Yehudi Bulgariyah Bishanot Hamishpat Hanatsi, 1940-1944* (The Jews of Bulgaria during Nazi occupation, 1940-1944), is representative of the articles insisting on the central role played by the king. Articles that emphasize the role played by public opinion and the resistance movement include Vladislav Topalov "L' Opinion publique Bulgare contre les persécutions des Juifs (Octombre 1940-9 Septembre 1944)" (Bulgarian public opinion against the persecution of the Jews), in *Etudes historiques a l' occasion du XXIIe Congrès International des Sciences Historiques*, 1965; Matei Yulzari, "The Bulgarian Jews in the Resistance Movement", in *They Fought Back: The Story of the Jewish Resistance in Nazi Europe*, edited by Yuri Suhl, 275-81; Albert Koen, *Saving of the Jews in Bulgaria, 1941-1944*, which is a government publication; and Uri Oren, "A Town Called Monastir: The Heroes", in *Anthology on Armed Jewish Resistance, 1939-1945* edited by Isaac Kowalski, a book that highlights the role of certain individuals in the resistance movement.

The destruction of the Jews in the territories occupied by Bulgaria is examined in Nadejda Slavi Vasileva, "On the Catastrophe of the Thracian Jews", and Aleksander Matkovsky, "The Destruction of Macedonian Jewry", both in *Yad Vashem Studies on the European Catastrophe and Resistance* 3 (1959), and Hans Joachim Hoppe, "Germany, Bulgaria, Greece: Their Relations and Bulgarian Policy in Occupied Greece", *Journal of the Hellenic Diaspora* 11 (Fall 1984): 41-54.

Greece

The case of neighboring Greece is different from that of Bulgaria. After a six-month war against Italy and then Germany, Greece was occupied by the Axis forces in May 1941. The Nazis, however, only retained control of several strategic points in the country, including Thessaloniki, leaving the rest to the Italians and the northeastern area of Greece to the Bulgarians. A Quisling government was intsalled in Athens. The harshness of the Axis occupation soon produced a Communist-led resistance movement in the mountain areas.

The Nazi authorities introduced a number of anti-Semitic measures in Thessaloniki, where the great majority of Greek Jews resided. But actual arrests and deportations were begun as late as March 1943. Nonetheless, by virtue of their military control of the area, the Nazis easily rounded up almost the entire Jewish population of the city. They were assisted in their task by the fact that they managed to persuade the community's chief rabbi of their supposed good intentions toward the Jews. Having completed the deportation of Thessaloniki' s Jews by the summer of 1943, the Nazis turned their attention toward the other, smaller Jewish communities in Greece.

As most of the remaining Jewish communities were located in Italian-occupied Greece, the Nazis waited to proceed until the Italian capitulation of September 1943. Indeed, the Italians had been wholly uncooperative with their Nazi allies, steadfastly refusing to sanction anti-Jewish measures and in some cases even helping Jews avoid arrest by the Nazis. Following Italy's capitulation, however, the Germans assumed responsibility for administering the whole of occupied Greece (with the exception of the Bulgarian zone in the northeast) and moved against the remaining Jewish communities.

The Nazis were only partially successful in rounding

up the remaining Jewish communities, failing to do so in towns that were accessible to the resistance movement and where Jews were more assimilated than they had been in Thessaloniki and were thus indistinguishable from the rest of the population. The majority of Jews living in the cities of Athens and Volos and on the island of Zakinthos survived largely thanks to the help proffered by the resistance movement, Greek officials, and the Orthodox church. Nonetheless, communities were totally destroyed. At the end of the war 62,573 Jews had lost their lives out of a total Jewish population of 79,950; over 46,000 of those who died were Thessaloniki Jews.

The standard, though now somewhat dated, work on the Holocaust in Greece remains the book by Michael Molho and Joseph Nehama, *In Memoriam: The Destruction of Greek Jewry* (more recent revised editions exist in French and Greek). It presents an overall picture of the Holocaust in Greece. The authors appear reluctant to underline the role played by the resistance movement. Steven Bowman, "Jews in Wartime Greece", *Jewish Social Studies* 49 (Winter 1986): 45-61, offers an updated and balanced overview based on extensive research. Bowman has also published a bibliographic guide to work on the Jews in wartime Greece in *Greece in the 1940s: A Nation in Crisis,* edited by John O. Iatrides, 83-94.

Studies on the assistance proffered by the resistance movement, the church and Greek officials include L. S. Stavrianos, "The Jews of Greece", *Journal of Central European Affairs 8* (October 1948); Avram Elmaleh, *Les*

Juifs de Salonique et la résistance hellénique (The Jews of Thessaloniki and the Greek Resistance); and Alexandros Kitroeff, "Greek Wartime Attitudes Towards the Jews in Athens", *Forum* 60 (Summer 1987): 41-51, where a direct link is drawn between the degree of Jewish assimilation and the effectiveness of the local resistance movement, on the one hand, and the salvation of the Jews of Athens, on the other, and "Documents: The Jews in Greece, 1941-1944: Eyewitness Accounts", *Journal of the Hellenic Diaspora* 12 (Fall 1985): 5-32.

As was the case in Bulgaria and Yugoslavia, a number of Jews participated in the Greek resistance movement. A spate of recent publications in Greece on the wartime resistance contains several references on this subject. Among the non-Greek sources, see Isaac Kabelli, "The Resistance of the Greek Jews", *YIVO Annual of Jewish Social Sciences* 8 (1953): 281-88; and Asher Moisses, "Jews in the Army of Greece", in *Ha-Lohhem ha-Yehudi be-Seva' ot ha-' Olam* (The Jewish fighter in the armies of the world).

The reluctance of Italian forces to implement anti-Semitic measures and arrest Jews is covered in Jacques Sabille, "Attitude of the Italians to the Jews in Occupied Greece", in *Jews Under the Italian Occupation*, edited by Leon Poliakov and Jacques Sabille, 151-60; and Susan Zuccotti, *The Italians and the Holocaust: Persecution, Rescue, and Survival*, 74-100, which al-so briefly mentions Italian policy in Croatia. The assistance of the Spanish government, which offered Sephardic Jews Spanish nationality, was another important factor contributing to the salvation of the Greek Jews. See Haim Avni, "Spanish Nationals in Greece and Their Fate During the Holocaust", *Yad Vashem Studies* 8 (1970): 31-68, and his book, *Spain, Franco, and the Jews.*

The questions surrounding the role of Thessaloniki's chief rabbi, Zvi Koretz, are complicated and still unclear. The view in the standard work on the Holocaust in Greece by Molho and Nehama (*In Memoriam,* cited earlier) is that if Zvi Koretz was not a "collaborator", he was at the least guilty of assisting the Germans. This view has been challenged by Nathan Eck, "New Light on the Charges Against the Last Grand Rabbi of Salonica", *Yad Vashem Bulletin* 17 (1965): 9-15; and by Joseph Ben, "Jewish Leadership in Greece During the Holocaust", in *Patterns of the Jewish Leadership in Nazi Europe,* edited by Yisrael Gutman and Cynthia Haft. While Eck seeks to exonerate the rabbi, Ben suggests that the rabbi was guilty of naiveté rather than collaboration. For an assessment of the role of the rabbi in Ioannina, see Rachel Dalven, "The Holocaust in Jannina", *Journal of Modern Greek Studies* 2 (May 1984): 87-103.

Memoirs and eyewitness accounts of the Nazi death camps include Danid Benveniste, *Yehudei Saloniki be-doroth ha-aharonim* (Thessaloniki Jewry in recent generations); Albert Menasche, *Birkenau (Auschwitz II): How 72,000 Greek Jews Perished;* and Errikos Sevillias, *Athens, Auschwitz.*

Romania

The quasi-Fascist Romanian dictatorship (1937-38) and the royal dictatorship (1939-40) were both responsible for increasing anti-Semitic measures in that country. In September 1940 Marshal Ion Antonescu became dictator, sharing power with the Fascist, terrorist Iron Guard. An office of "Romanization" was subsequently established to transfer Jewish, Greek, and Armenian property into Romanian hands; Jewish agricultural property was confiscated; and Jews employed in commerce and industry were dismissed. Forever the scapegoat for the country's problems, some 120 Jews were killed and their bodies hung in a Bucharest slaughterhouse during an Iron Guard uprising against Antonescu. Backed by the army, Antonescu soon eliminated the Iron Guard and established total control over Romania.

Worse suffering was to follow for the Jews in Bessarabia and Northern Bukovina. Falsely accusing the Jews of having welcomed the Soviets in those areas in 1940, the Antonescu regime turned against the Bessarabian and Bukovinan Jews with unprecedented brutality, even by Romanian standards. With the help of German troops, a pogrom in the town of Jassy took place in the summer of 1941. About 8,000 Jews were killed, some of them dying in closed cattle cars that were shunted from place to place. Mass shootings claimed a total of 100,000 Jewish lives.

The remaining Jews of these regions were sent to Trans-Dnistria, an area on the Romanian-Ukrainian border between the Dniester and Bug rivers. Of the 185,000 deported Bessarabian and Bukovinan Jews only about 30,000 avoided suffering a slow death in inhuman conditions that rivalled those of the Nazi death camps. All told, 380,000 Romanian Jews lost their lives in Bessarabia, Northern Bukovina, and Trans-Dnistria.

Yet despite Nazi wishes, the 350,000 Jews in central Romania ("Old" or Regat Romania) were not deported. Although the Nazis did eventually reach an agreement with the Romanian regime that would have allowed deportations to begin in September 1942, ultimately these did not take place. The battle waged by Jewish community leaders in Bucharest and by the influential and proassimilationist Dr. Wilhelm Filderman bore fruit. Conditions in Trans-Dnistria were alleviated and deportations from "Old" Romania were delayed. Furthermore, the Romanian regime did not want to be regarded as merely a Nazi satellite and was thus in no hurry to comply with Nazi plans. When the Nazis began suffering setbacks in the war, the deportation plan was abandoned.

A large collection of documents relating to the Holocaust in Romania, Jean Ancel, *Documents Concerning the Fate of Romanian Jewry During the Holocaust*, provides researchers with very useful material. General overviews of events in Romania include Stephen Fischer-Galati, "Fascism, Communism, and the Jewish Question in Romania", in *Jews and Non-Jews in Eastern Europe, 1918-1945*, edited by Bela Vago and George L. Mosse.

Most works on the plight of the Jews in wartime Romania focus on the destruction wrought in the northern areas rather than on the situation in "Old" Romania. Studies on Trans-Dnistria include Joseph B. Schechtman, "The Trans-Dnistria Reservation", *YIVO Annual* 8 (1953): 178-96; Meier Teich, "The Jewish Self-Administration in Ghetto Shargorod (Trans-Dnistria)" *Yad Vashem Studies* 2 (1952): 219-54; Dora Litani, "'Courier', an Underground Newspaper in Trans-Dnistria, April-September 1943", *Yad Vashem Bulletin* 14 (March 1964): 44-48; Julius S. Fisher, *Trans-Dnistria: The Forgotten Cemetery*; and Bela Vago, "The Destruction of the Jews of Transylvania", *Hungarian Jewish Studies* 1 (1966): 171-221.

Among those works that focus on the Jewish leadership's efforts to counter anti-Semitic measures in "Old" Romania and the help offered by non-Jews, see Theodore Lavi, "Documents on the Struggle of Romanian Jewry for Its Rights During the Second World War", *Yad Vashem Studies* 4 (1960): 274-75, "The Background to the Rescue of Romanian Jewry During the Period of the Holocaust", in *Jews and Non-Jews in Eastern Europe,* 1918-1945, edited by Bela Vago and George L. Mosse, and "The Vatican's Endeavors on Behalf of Romanian Jewry During the Second World War", *Yad Vashem Studies* 5 (1960): 414. See also Bela Vago, "The Ambiguity of Collaborationism: The Center of the Jews in Romania (1942-1944)", in *Patterns of the Jewish Leadership in Nazi Europe, 1939-1945: Proceedings of the Third Yad Vashem International Historical Conference,* edited by Yisrael Gutman and Cynthia

J. Haft, where Vago outlines the leadership's dual role, simultaneous collaboration with the authorities and assistance to the Jews.

For the role played by the resistance movement-a factor of secondary importance in Romania-see A. Artzi, "The Underground Activities of the Pioneer Movements in Romania During World War II", *Yad Vashem Bulletin* 12 (1962): 34-41. A very useful eyewitness account is Emil Dorian, *The Quality of Witness: A Romanian Diary, 1937-1944*, with an informative introduction by Michael Stanislawski that sketches the historical background.

The Jews of Northern Transylvania, who had suffered during the interwar period at the hands of the anti-Semitic Romanian state, found themselves under Hungarian rule during the war, since their region was transferred to Hungary by the Nazis. The bitter irony was that while the Jews had welcomed Hungarian rule, traditionally more sympathetic to the Jews than Romanian rule, they were rounded up and deported in the final stages of the war, when the Hungarians eventually relented in the face of Nazi pressures. A study by Nathaniel Katzburg, *Hungary and the Jews: Policy and Legislation, 1920-1943*, provides one of the most useful general accounts of Hungarian Jewish policy during the war. On the Northern Transylvania Jews, see R. L. Braham, ed., *Genocide and Retribution: An Aspect of the Holocaust in Hungary*, and Bela Vago, "Political and Diplomatic Activities for the Rescue of the Jews of Northern Transylvania, June 1944-February 1945", *Yad Vashem Studies* 6 (1967): 155-73. Bela Vago's "Contrasting Jewish Leadership in Wartime

Hungary and Romania" in *The Holocaust as Historical Experience*, edited by Yehuda Bauer and Nathan Rotenstreich, also provides a useful comparison between Hungarian and Romanian policies.

Yugoslavia

Occupied by Axis forces in April 1941, Yugoslavia was partitioned and ceased to exit as a unified state. Germany occupied Slovenia, the Banat, and Serbia (the northern and central areas of the country); Italy occupied Dalmatia on the western coast and several inland regions; Hungary occupied a northeastern area of Yugoslavia; and Bulgaria occupied the southern province of Vardar. Finally, Croatia, in the north, became an independent entity administered by the Ustasha, a Croatian Fascist organization.

As early as May 1941, preliminary measures were taken against the twelve thousand Serbian Jews. A few months later, roundups and shootings of Jews began in earnest both in Serbia and the Banat region. Death camps were established within Serbia by the occupation forces and those interned were either shot or killed in gas vans. By mid-1942 the destruction of the Jews in Serbia and the Banat was completed.

In Croatia the Ustasha implemented anti-Jewish measures with a Nazi-like determination. Roundups of Croatian and Bosnian Jews began in 1941 to camps like Jasenovac. Those who did not die of hardships endured in the Croatian camps, about nine thousand, were eventually deported to Auschwitz. The eight thousand Jews living in Bulgarian-occupied territories were also deported in March 1943, while Jews in the Hungarian-occupied territories were deported by mid-1944.

Only Jews living in areas under Italian control, and those who managed to make their way to those areas, were able to avoid deportation. The Italians did not deport Jews to Germany and Poland, although they did intern Jews in those areas within their jurisdiction. As in Greece after Italy's capitulation in September 1943, Nazi forces moved in and deported a number of Jews, but many either escaped to Italy or joined the partisan resistance movement.

The Yugoslav partisan movement was not strong enough to prevent or even frustrate deportations of Jews, as had been the case in Greece. Deportations were in fact carried out long before the Yugoslav resistance movement had time to organize. There are some works on the important role played by the Jews in the Yugoslav resistance movement. There are no studies, however, on public attitudes during the roundups, with the main bulk of work focusing on the details of the roundups and deportations in Serbia and Croatia.

Studies by Zdenko Lowenthal, ed., *The Crimes of the Fascist Occupants and Their Collaborators Against Jews in Yugoslavia*, and Jasa Romano *Jews of Yugoslavia, 1941-1945: Victims of Genocide and Freedom Fighters*, provide an overall picture of the events in Yugoslavia, including the role that Jews played in the resistance movement. Charles W. Steckel, "Survivors and Partisans", and Uri Oren, "A Town Called Monastir", both in *Anthology on Armed Jewish Resistance, 1939-1945*, edited by Isaac Kowalski, are also worth consulting.

The fate of the Serbian Jews is accounted for in Nathan Eck, "The March of Death from Serbia to Hungary (September 1994)", *Yad Vashem Studies* 2 (1958): 255-94. The fate of the Croatian Jews is related in Yeshayahu Jelinek, "The Holocaust of Croatian Jewry: A Few Reflections", *Shoah* 1 (1979): 20-23; and Edmond Paris, *Genocide in Satellite Croatia, 1941-1945: A Record of Racial and Religious Persecutions and Massacres.* Finally, Jacques Sabille's "The Attitude of the Italians to the Persecuted Jews in Croatia", in *Jews Under the Italian Occupation,* edited by Leon Poliakov and Jacques Sabille, 129-50, examines the role of the Italian forces in Croatia during the war.

The Balkans and Holocaust Historiography

Eastern European Jews suffered the greatest losses during the Holocaust, and studies have thus naturally tended to focus more on Eastern than on Western Europe. But Southeastern Europe, the Balkans — with the exception of Romania, which is often considered part of Eastern Europe — has been even more neglected in Holocaust studies than Western Europe.

The most systematic treatment of the Holocaust in Balkan countries can be found in Raul Hilberg, *The Destruction of the European Jews* (originally published in 1951 and revised in 1978), pages 432-554, which also includes Hungary and Slovakia as part of the Balkans. In this masterful overview of the Holocaust in Europe, the author is primarily concerned with *how* rather than *why* questions and deals with the gruesome process of discrimination, arrest, and deportation. Hilberg outlines these processes in a detailed manner, basing his research on German documents that provide new and valuable insights on events in the Balkan countries. In addition, although only in passing, Hilberg offers some comparisons between the deportation process in the Balkan countries and that which occurred elsewhere in Europe.

Written with the intention of refuting theories of Jewish passivity, Nora Levin's *The Holocaust: The Destruction of European Jewry, 1933-1945* includes in the second part of the book, short chapters on each of the Balkan countries. These examine wartime Jewish-Gentile relations and Jewish participation in local resistance movements and are based on several available secondary sources. The most representative work of earlier studies that have been criticized for stressing Jewish passivity is Gerald Reitlinger's *The Final Solution: The Attempt to Exterminate the Jews of Europe, 1939-1945* (2d revised and augmented edition). Reitlinger's sections on the Balkan counties are informative-Yugoslavia, 385-98: Greece, 398-408; Bulgaria, 408-14; Romania, 425-46; and Hungarian-occupied Romania, 454-71.

Also useful is Martin Gilbert's *The Holocaust: A History of the Jews of Europe During the Second World War*, a chronological account of the Holocaust that combines archival, published, and oral sources. There are references to the fate of the Jews in each of the

Balkan countries throughout this book.

Insofar as general interpretations are concerned, the explanation of the Holocaust as a preconceived Nazi plan has many adherents. The most representative general work of this so-called internationalist school is Lucy S. Dawidowicz's *The War Against the Jews, 1933-1945* (originally published in 1975). The author suggests that the Nazis engaged in two parallel "wars", one against the countries of Europe and another against the Jews, which they had systematically planned earlier on. At the end of the book Dawidowicz includes short descriptions of the fate of the Jews in each European country, including the Balkans (Romania, 383-86; Bulgaria, 386-90; Yugoslavia, 390-92; Greece, 392-94). These accounts, however, whose brevity does not permit any reference to sources, focus exclusively on measures taken against the Jews. No mention is made of parallel repressive measures against others, such as those adopted against Serbians in Croatia, or against Armenians and Greeks as well as Jews as a result of the early "romanization of property" legislation in Romania. Finally, the specific wartime experiences of the Balkan Jews do not furnish a great deal of evidence for Dawidowicz's main argument. Indeed, only in Yugoslavia was the Jewish question addressed early on by the Nazis. Arrests of Greek Jews began almost two years after Greece fell to the Axis, while pressure applied to the Bulgarians and Romanians to deport their Jewish populations came too late. It would seem, therefore, that not all Balkan Jewish experiences conform to the intentionalist thesis of a preplanned "war against the Jews".

The so-called intentionalist school has come under criticism by writers who have stressed the functional aspects of the roundups, shootings, and deportations, depicting the Third Reich as a maze of competing power groups rather than a well-oiled machine totally under Hitler's control. The arguments and debates between the two sides are more relevant to the study of Nazi wartime policy as a whole than to the study of the Holocaust per se. If indeed the Third Reich was much less a programmed, well-oiled machine than has been seen by some, it is important that Holocaust historiography take into full account the involvement of other actors involved, such as the collaborationist governments, resistance movements, and the general public. One way of assessing these other factors is by examining the issue of Gentile-Jewish relations. While underlining the importance of German anti-Semitism, Yehuda Bauer has focused on the subject of Gentile-Jewish relations in *The Holocaust in Historical Perspective.* He examines those relations in the Balkans on pages 63-67. Bauer also briefly assesses the Holocaust in Romania in *A History of the Holocaust,* pages 305-9. Bauer's conclusion, that German and Polish Jews were offered little assistance in their hour of need by ordinary people in communities where the Jews had lived in relative isolation, also hold true for Greece. The Greek public was much more helpful to the more assimilated Jewish communities than it was to the less assimilated communities. This hypothesis is one well worth pursuing in examining the cases of other Balkan countries.

The Balkan experience could also be integrated into mainstream studies of the Holocaust along the line of argumentation recently suggested by Michael Marru's *The Holocaust in History.* The author's aim is to study the Holocaust in much the same way that other historical phenomena are studied and interpreted, without, nonetheless, denying the "unique" and "humanly unimaginable" dimensions upon which earlier works on the Holocaust have insisted. Marrus examines the whole gamut of anti-Semitic policies, arrests, shootings, deportations, and destruction of the Holocaust against the background of overall wartime Nazi strategy. He then explains why the Holocaust should not be studied in isolation from other aspects of Nazi policy during the war by furnishing ample evidence of the often haphazard and uneven development of Nazi policy toward the Jews across occupied Europe, including the Balkans. The Balkans, in fact, offer as fertile terrain as any in which to test Marrus's approach. The Nazis adopted vastly different approaches to the Jewish question in each of the Balkan countries. General Nazi strategy differed both in the two collaborationist states of Bulgaria and Romania and in the two occupied states, Greece and Yugoslavia. These differences in Nazi policies contributed to the contrasts in the wartime experiences of the Jewish communities in the Balkan countries. Future research on the Jewish communities in the Balkans could profitably address this question, in addition to the aforementioned issue of Gentile-Jewish relations. The richness of the Jewish experiences in the Balkan countries and their similarities and contrasts provide a useful testing ground in the development and srengthening of Holocaust historiography.

NOTES

1. Among the various bibliographies of the Holocaust, the most useful on the Balkans is Abraham J. Edelheit and Herschel Edelheit, eds., *Bibliography on Holocaust Literature* (Boulder, Colo.: Westview Press, 1986).

2. The standard works on nineteenth-century Balkan history include L. S. Stavrianos, *The Balkans, 1815-1914* (New York: Holt, Rinehart and Winston, 1963); Peter F. Sugar and Donald W. Treadgold, eds., *A History of East Central Europe*, vols. 5 and 8 (Seattle: University of Washington Press, 1977); and Barbara Jelavich, *History of the Balkans: Eighteenth and Nineteenth Centuries* (Cambridge, England: Cambridge University Press, 1983). See also Dimitrije Djordjevic and Stephen Fischer-Galati, *The Balkan Revolutionary Tradition* (New York: Columbia University Press, 1981).

3. For the history of minorities in the Balkans, see Raymond Pearson, *National Minorities in Eastern Europe, 1848-1945* (London: Macmillan, 1983).

4. James Fawcett, *The International Protection of Minorities*, Minority Rights Group Report no. 41 (London: MRG, 1979).

5. The standard account of interwar Balkan history remains Robert Lee Wolff, *The Balkans in Our Time* (New York: W. W. Norton, 1967).

SELECT BIBLIOGRAPHY

Ancel, Jean. *Documents Concerning the Fate of Romanian Jewry During the Holocaust.* Vols. 1-12. New York: Beate Klarsfeld Foundation, 1986.

Arditi, Benjamin. *Yehudi Bulgariyah Bishanot Hamishpat Hantasi, 1940-1944* (The Jews of Bulgaria during Nazi occupation, 1949-1944). Tel Aviv: Israel Press, 1962.

Artzi, A. "The Underground Activities of the Pioneer Movements in Romania During World War II". *Yad Vashem Bulletin* 12 (1962): 34-41.

Avni, Haim. *Spain, Franco, and the Jews.* Translated by E. Shimon: Philadelphia: Jewish Publication Society of America, 1982.

"Spanish Nationals in Greece and Their Fate During the Holocaust". *Yad Vashem Studies* 8 (1970): 31-68.

Bauer, Yehuda. *A History of the Holocaust.* New York: Franklin Watts, 1982.

The Holocaust in Historical Perspective. Seattle: University of Washington Press, 1978.

Ben, Joseph. "Jewish Leadership in Greece During the Holocaust". In *Patterns of the Jewish Leadership in Nazi Europe,* edited by Yisrael Gutman and Cynthia Haft. Jerusalem: Yad Vashem, 1977.

Benveniste, David. *Yehudei Saloniki be-doroth ha-aharonim* (Thessaloniki Jewry in recent generations). Jerusalem, 1973.

Bowman, Steven. "Jews in Wartime Greece". *Jewish Social Studies* 49 (Winter 1986): 45-61.

Braham, R. L., ed. *Genocide and Retribution: An Aspect of the Holocaust in Hungary.* Boston: Kluwer-Nijhoff, 1983.

Chary, Frederick B. *The Bulgarian Jews and the Final Solution, 1940-1944.* Pittsburgh: University of Pittsburgh

Press, 1972.

"The Bulgarian Writers' Protest of October 1940 Against the Introduction of Antisemitic Legislation into the Kingdom of Bulgaria". *East European Quarterly* 4 (March 1, 1970): 88-93.

Dalven, Rachel. "The Holocaust in Jannina". *Journal of Modern Greek Studies* 2 (May 1984): 87-103.

Dawidowicz, Lucy. *The War Against the Jews, 1933-1945.* New York: Holt, Rinehart and Winston, 1975.

Dorian Emil. *The Quality of Witness: A Romanian Diary, 1937-1944.* Edited by Marguerite Dorian. Philadelphia: Jewish Publication Society of America, 1982.

Eck, Nathan. "The March of Death from Serbia to Hungary (September 1944)". *Yad Vashen Studies* 2 (1958): 255-94.

"New Light on the Charges Against the Last Grand Rabbi of Salonica". *Yad Vashen Bulletin* 17 (1965): 9-15.

Elazar, Daniel J. "The Sunset of Balkan Jewry". *Forum* 27, no. 2 (1977): 135-41.

Elmaleh, Avram. *Les Juifs de Salonique et la réistance hellénique* (The Jews of Thessaloniki and the Greek resistance). Istanbul - Thessaloniki, 1949.

Emmanuel, I. S. *Histoire des Israélites de Salonique* (History of the Jews of Salonika). Paris: Thonon, 1936.

Fischer - Galati, Stephen. "Fascism, Communism, and the Jewish Question in Rumania". In *Jews and Non-Jews in Eastern Europe, 1918-1945,* edited by Bela Vago and George L. Mosse. Jerusalem: Israel Universities Press, 1974.

Fisher, Julius S. *Transdnistria: The Forgotten Cemetery.* South Brunswick: A. T. Yoseloff, 1969.

Freidenreich, Harriet Pass. *The Jews of Yugoslavia: A Quest for Community.* Philadelphia: Jewish Publication Society of America, 1979.

Galante, Abraham. *Documents officials Turcs concernant les juifs de Turquie* (Official Turkish documents concerning the Jews of Turkey). Istanbul: Haim, Rozio. 1931.

Gelber, N. M. "Jewish Life in Bulgaria". *Jewish Social Studies* 8 (1946): 103-26.

Gilbert, Martin. *The Holocaust: A History of the Jews of Europe During the Second World War*. New York: Henry Holt. 1985.

Hilberg, Raul. *The Destruction of the European Jews*. Rev. ed. New York: Octagon Books, 1978.

Hoppe, Hans Joachim. "Germany, Bulgaria, Greece: Their Relations and Bulgarian Policy in Occupied Greece". *Journal of the Hellenic Diaspora* 11 (Fall 1984): 41-54.

Iatrides, John O., ed. *Greece in the 1940s: A Nation in Crisis*. Hanover: University Press of New England, 1981, pp. 83-94.

Janowsky, Oscar I. *People at Bay: The Jewish Problem in East Central Europe*. New York: Oxford University Press, 1938.

Jelinek, Yeshayahu. "The Holocaust of Croatian Jewry : A Few Reflections". *Shoah* 1 (1979): 20-23.

Kabelli, Isaac. "The Resistance of the Greek Jews". *YIVO Annual of Jewish Social Sciences* 8 (1953): 281-88.

Katzbur, Nathnaniel. *Hungary and the Jews: Policy and Legislation, 1920-1943*. Ramat Gan: Bar Ilan University Press, 1981.

Kitroeff, Alexandros. "Documents: The Jews in Greece, 1941 - 1944: Eyewitness Accounts". *Journal of the Hellenic Diaspora* 12 (Fall 1985): 5-32.

"Greek Wartime Attitudes Towards the Jews in Athens". *Forum* 60 (Summer 1987): 41-51.

Koen, Albert. *Saving of the Jews in Bulgaria, 1941-1944*. Sofia: Setemvri, 1977.

Lavi, Theodore. "The Background to the Rescue of Romanian Jewry During the Period of the Holocaust". In *Jews and Non-Jews in Eastern Europe, 1918-1945*, edited by Bela Vago and George L. Mosse.

"Documents on the Struggle of Rumanian Jewry for its Rights During the Second War". *Yad Vashem Studies 5* (1960): 274 - 75.

"Vatican Endeavors on Behalf of Rumanian Jewry During the Second World War". *Yad Vashem Studies 5* (1963): 405-18.

Levin, Nora. *The Holocaust: The Destruction of European Jewry, 1933-1945*. New York: Crowell, 1968.

Lewis, Bernard. *The Jews of Islam*. London: Routledge and Kegan Paul, 1984.

Litani, Dora. "'Courier', an Underground Newspaper in Trans-Dnistria, April - September 1943". *Yad Vashem Bulletin* 14 (March 1964): 44-48.

Lowenthal, Zdenko, ed. *The Crimes of the Fascist Occupants and Their Callaborators Against Jews in Yugoslavia*. Belgrade: Federation of Jewish Communities, 1957.

Marrus, Michael. *The Holocaust in History*. Hanover, N. H.: University Press of New England, 1987.

Matkovsky, Aleksandar. "The Destruction of Macedonian Jewry". *Yad Vashem Studies on the European Catastrophe and Resistance 3* (1959): 211-13.

Mavrogordatos, George Th. *Stillborn Republic: Social Coalitions and Party Strategies in Greece, 1922-1936*. Berkeley: University of California Press, 1983.

Menasche, Albert. *Birkenau (Auschwitz II): How 72,000 Greek Jews Perished*. New York, Saltiel 1947.

Mendelsohn, Ezra. *The Jews of East Central Europe Between the World Wars*. Bloomington: Indiana University Press, 1983.

Mezan, Saul. *Les Juifs Espagnols en Bulgarie* (The Spanish Jews in Bulgaria). Sofia: Amiscpat, 1925.

Miller, Marshall L. *Bulgaria During the Second World War*. Stanford, Calif.: Stanford University Press, 1975.

Moisses, Asher. "Jews in the Army of Greece". In *Ha-Lohhem ha-Yehudi be-Seva'ot ha-Olam* (The Jewish fighter in the armies of the world). Tel Aviv, 1967.

Molho, Michael. *Usos y costumbres de los Sefardies de Salonica* (Habits and customs of the Sephardim in Salonika). Madrid and Barcelona: Instituto Arias Montano, Consejo Superior de Investigaciones Cientificas, 1950.

Molho, Michael, and Joseph Nehama. *In Memoria: The Destruction of Greek Jewry*. Jerusalem: Jewish Community of Salonika, 1956.

Nehama, Joseph. *Histoire des Israélites de Salonique.* (History of the Jews of Salonika). Vols. 6 and 7. Thessaloniki: Jewish Community of Thessaloniki, 1978.

Oren, Nissan. "The Bulgarian Exception: A Reassessment of the Salvation of the Jewish Community". *Yad Vashem Studies on the European Jewish Catastrophe and Resistance* 13 (1969): 83-106.

Oren, Uri. "A Town Called Monastir: The Heroes". In *Anthology on Armed Jewish Resistance, 1939-1945*, edited by Isaac Kowalski. New York: Shapolsky, 1988.

Paris, Edmond. *Genocide in Satellite Croatia, 1931-1945: A Record of Racial and Religious Persecutions and Massacres*. Chicago: American Institute for Balkan Affairs, 1961.

Reitlinger, Gerald. *The Final Solution: The Attempt to Exterminate the Jews of Europe, 1939-1945*. 2d rev. ed. N. Y.: T. Yoseloff, 1968.

Romano, A., Joseph Ben, and Nisim (Buko) Levy. *Yehudut Bulgariyah* (the Jewish of Bulgaria). Jerusalem: Encyclopedia of the Jewish Diaspora Co., 1968.

Romano, Jasa. *Jews of Yugoslavia, 1941-1945: Victims of Genocide and Freedom Fighters.* Belgrade: Federation of Jewish Communities of Yugoslavia, 1982.

Sabille, Jacques. "Attitude of the Italians to the Jews in Occupied Greece". In *Jews Under the Italian Occupation,* edited by Leon Poliakov and Jacques Sabille, pp. 151-60. New York: Howard Fertig, 1983.

"The Attitude of the Italians to the Persecuted Jews in Croatia". In *Jews Under the Italian Occupation,* pp. 129-50.

Schechtman, Joseph. "The Transdnistria Reservation". *YIVO Annual* 8 (1953): 178-96.

Sciaky, Leon. *Farewell to Salonica.* New York: Current Books, 1946.

Sevillias, Errikos. *Athens, Auschwitz.* Translated by Nikos Stavroulakis. Athens: Lycabettus Press, 1983.

Stavrianos, L. S. "The Jews of Greece". *Journal of Central European Affairs* 8 (October 1948).

Steckel, Charles. "Survivors and Partisans". In *Anthology on Armed Jewish Resistance, 1939-1945,* edited by Isaac Kowalski. Vol. 1.

Teich, Meier. "The Jewish Self-Administration in Ghetto Shargorod (Trans-Dnistria)". *Yad Vashem Studies* 2 (1952): 219-54.

Topalov, Vladislav. "L' Opinion publique Bulgare contre les persécutions des Juifs (October 1940-9 September 1944)" (Bulgarian public opinion against the persecutions of the Jews). In *Etudes historiques à l' occasion du XXIIe Congrès International des Sciences Historiques, 1965.* Sofia: BAN, 1965.

Vago, Bela. "The Ambiguity of Collaborationism: The Center of the Jews in Romania (1942-1944)". In *Patterns of the Jewish Leadership in Nazi Europe, 1939-1945: Proceedings of the Third Yad Vashem International Historical Con-*

ference, edited by Yisrael Gutman and Cynthia Haft.

"Contrasting Jewish Leadership in Wartime Hungary and Romania". In *The Holocaust as Historical Experience,* edited by Yehuda Bauer and Nathan Rotenstreich. New York: Holmes and Meier, 1981.

"The Destruction of the Jews of Transylvania". *Hungarian Jewish Studies* I (1966): 171-221.

"Political and Diplomatic Activities for the Rescue of the Jews of Northern Transylvania. June 1944-February 1945". *Yad Vashem Studies* 6 (1967): 155-73.

Vasileva, Nadejda Slavi. "On the Catastrophe of the Thracian Jews". *Yad Vashem Studies on the European Catastrophe and Resistance* 2 (1959): 97.

Yulzari, Matei. "The Bulgarian Jews in the Resistance Movement". In *They Fought Back: The Story of the Jewish Resistance in Nazi Europe,* edited by Yuri Suhl. pp. 275-81. New York: Crown, 1967.

Zuccotti, Susan. *The Italians and the Holocaust: Persecution, Rescue, and Survival.* New York: Basic Books, 1987.

GREEK WAR-TIME ATTITUDES
TOWARDS THE JEWS IN ATHENS

In WW II, the Greek Jews shared the fate of their European brethren. The Axis occupation of Greece between 1941 and 1944 caused the most serious upheaval in the long history of the Jewish settlements within the present-day borders of Greece. In round figures 65,000 of a total of 80,000 in Greece perished during the Axis occupation. A number of studies and eyewitness accounts have focused on the annihilation of Greek Jews. Chronologically, the earliest published material dealt with the round-ups, deportations and events in the camps. Following Greece's return to parliamentary democracy in 1974, a flood of books and articles on the Greek Resistance movement were issued, several of which mentioned the contributions of Greek Jews. Most of this body of information has been itemized in a comprehensive bibliography on the Jews during the resistance period.[1] Official state recognition of the left-wing resistance organizations in 1982 occasioned a number of articles in *Chronica* describing the part the Jews played in these organizations.[2]

Meanwhile, a few monographs have appeared addressing specific issues related to the wartime history of the Greek Jews.[3] One important issue is the attitude towards the Jews of the rest of the population in war-time Greece. In his essay "Jew and Gentile: The Holocaust and After", Yehuda Bauer wrote:

> Even a cursory glance at the available information makes it clear that one of the more important determinants of the fate of European Jewry during the Holocaust was the attitude towards them of their non — Jewish neighbors. Protection given to Jews by the peoples conquered by the Nazis was in many cases life — saving. Absence of such protection left the Jews to the mercies of the SS murderers and their collaborators from among the other European nations. We are therefore dealing not with a historical footnote, but with a central historical problem...[4]

This article hopes to contribute towards a better understanding of the political and social factors which influenced the attitudes of Greek Gentiles towards the Jews. On the basis of the experiences of the Jews in Athens, it will be argued that two important factors were the degree of assimilation of the Jewish community in each area and the level of the national resistance movement in the same area.

On the eve of WW II, over 70% of Greek Jews lived in Thessaloniki while the remainder formed several much smaller communities. The largest was in Athens (3,500 people) followed by Kavala (2,200), Corfu (2.000), Jannina (1,950), Drama (1,200), Larissa (1,175), Kastoria (900), Volos (882) and a few even smaller ones.[5]

Of these, the Athens community was one of the few which escaped destruction. Before examining developments in Athens, a brief chronology of Nazi measures against the Greek Jews is in order.[6] These measures were not enforced simultaneously on a national scale because of Greece's division into three zones of occupation: German, Italian and Bulgarian. The Athens Jews remained under Italian jurisdiction until September 1943 and were included in plans for the "Final Solution" after this date. The process of destroying Greek Jewry began relatively late. Deportations from Thessaloniki commenced in the spring of 1943. The earlier discriminatory measures enforced against the Thessaloniki Jews had led many of them to move to Athens. During the time which elapsed between the deportations in Thessaloniki and September 1943, a number of Jews from other communities had also sought refuge in Athens. Thus, the total number of Jews in Athens had more than doubled reaching a figure of about 8,000.

Shortly after occupying Thessaloniki the German authorities arrested the Jewish Council (April 1941). In July 1942 all males between 18 and 45 were ordered to register for forced labor and subsequently about 3,000 were sent to parts of the country to work on road construction. In early 1943 all but a few foreign Jews were forced to identify themselves with yellow stars and their businesses with notices to the effect that these were Jewish-owned. A ghetto was formed and deportations began in February and in March. By August 1943 about 46,000 Thessaloniki Jews had been deported. This figure represented over 80 percent of the city's Jewish population. Meanwhile, deportations from Kavala, Drama and other Jewish centers under Bulgarian occupation took place in March 1943. The "Final Solution" was delayed in the other parts of Greece because these fell within the Italian zone of occupation. The Italians were steadfast in their refusal to cooperate with the Nazi plans for the Jews. After the Italian armistice in September 1943, the Italian zone of occupation in Greece was taken over by the Germans. In October the growing number of Jews in Athens were ordered to register; lack of response and inability of the authorities to locate the Jews caused large scale confiscation of property. In March 1944 a number of raids were carried out in Athens and the provincial towns yielding 5,500 Jews mainly form Jannina and Corfu, who were deported.

It seems reasonable to assume that the attitude of the other Greeks towards their persecuted Jewish compatriots depended a great deal on how far the Jews had been assimilated into Greek society. Bauer's comments on this with respect to other European countries are particularly enlightening:

> A comparison of Nazi policies against the Jews in different European countries will show that extreme steps against the Jews were successful wherever the Nazis succeeded in breaking off all contact between their victims and the non-Jewish environment. This was certainly true of western and central Poland, where the ghettos were shut off from the Polish surroundings

— whether hermetically as in the city of Lodz, or almost so in Warsaw or Lublin. Research now going on at the Institute für Zeitgeschichte in Munich, investigating the conversion of the Bavarian peasantry to Nazi antisemitism, has come to a similar conclusion: as long as the Jewish traders and peasants in the Bavarian countryside were part and parcel of a traditional scheme of social relationships, the peasants would not be persuaded by Nazi ideology. The change came after the Nazis had succeeded in isolating the Jews and had turned them into mysterious strangers living their lives at the end of the village.[7]

What one ought to bear in mind in the case of Greece is that with the exception of Athens, the main Jewish settlements referred to above had only recently been incorporated within the Greek state as a result of the annexation of Thessaly in 1880 and of the Balkan Wars in 1912-13. Moreover, these Jewish communities previously existed as independent entities within the multi-ethnic Ottoman Empire, with its tradition of religious tolerance. At the time when towns like Larissa, Volos, Jannina, Thessaloniki and Kavala became part of the Greek state, their Jewish communities were not only culturally isolated but physically separate. Stavroulakis mentions that:

> In most of the mainland towns there were Jewish quarters, not as consequence of a ghetto policy, but the natural tendency by the Jews throughout the centuries to consolidate their

lives near a synagogue.[8]

The cultural isolation grew more pronounced after these towns came under Greek control. While Turks, Bulgarians and other non-Greeks had the option of moving into areas not under Greek control (and thousands were forcibly moved in the exchange of populations in 1923 between Greece and Turkey), the Jews had no choice but to stay put, since they had no affiliation with any of the Balkan nations. They remained in an increasingly Greek environment to which they were distinctly alien: their communities were made up largely of Sephardic Jews who had retained their Judeo-Hispanic culture. Leon Sciaky has written of the Ottoman Jews that:

> Their language, somewhat corrupted by the admixture of the various dialects of their country of origin, and by the introduction of Turkish and Greek words, still remained distinctly Castillian of the sixteenth century ... it was a startling and naively joyful surprise to Senior Angel Pulido, a Spanish senator who visited Turkey in 1904, to discover not only could he converse freely in his mother tongue, but that he felt very much at home among the descendants of the people his forefathers had dealt with so brutally.[9]

The northern, Sephardic communities which had consciously resisted their assimilation into Ottoman and later Greek society were at a serious disadvantage in the face of the Nazi threat. They were more easily identified, isolated and discriminated against by the Occupation authorities despite the moral or political obligation among the Gentiles to come to their aid. The cultural division was a wide one. This is perhaps why several community leaders, well aware of this situation, chose to come to an arrangement with the Nazi authorities — a policy doomed to failure. Joseph Ben, in an important article on the policy of the Jewish leadership in wartime Greece, enumerates the "objective difficulties that prevented escape or attempts to rescue large numbers of Jews" in Thessaloniki and includes the near impossibility to conceal one's Jewish identity. He mentions that while a few of the younger generation could speak Greek, those over fifty years old "could scarcely stammer a few words in the local dialect." The author is critical of the community leadership's parleying with the Germans,[10] as is Rachel Dalven in her article on the destruction of another "isolated" community, that of Jannina.[11]

By contrast, the Jewish community in Athens was heterogeneous in its origin: Romanian, Ashkenazi and Sephardic. Its assimilation was not without problems in the 19th century (due to local hostility though, over the "Don Pacifico Affair")[12] but the tiny Jewish community went almost unnoticed in the 20th century city. The integration achieved by the community, its hellenization as a result of its heterogeneity, its small size and long existence in an exclusively Greek environment guaranteed anonymity during the war. It also made protection of incoming refugees easier because contacts with non-Jews were long established by the Athens

Jews and networks for aiding them were being set up as soon as Nazi discrimination in Thessaloniki became known.

Is the assimilation factor perhaps exaggerated in the present context? Might it have been discrimination by the Greeks against the Jews in the interwar period which spilt over into the war years and contributed to the destruction of Greek Jewry by the Nazis? There is no doubt that the Jews in Thessaloniki and elsewhere in the southern Ottoman Balkans were, on the whole, not interfered with and led a peaceful existence with many of them becoming prosperous. There is also no doubt that sooner or later these communities would have to come up against one or another variety of nationalism which began to spread in the Balkans in the 19th century. It was probably fortunate for the Jews of Thessaloniki and those in the surrounding areas that the nationalism they had to face was the Greek one. The pre-WW II antisemitism of other Balkan states, notably Romania and Bulgaria, is well known.[13] The historian L. S. Stavrianos has indicated that the Jews were better off in Greece than in other Eastern European countries on the eve of WW II.[14] But this is not to imply that interwar Greece can be absolved of antisemitism. In the absence of any scholarly work on antisemitism in pre-WW II Greece, the following rule-of-thumb designation of antisemitic manifestations may be proposed here for the purposes of this article:

a) religious antisemitism sponsored by the Orthodox Church,
b) political antisemitism on the part of political parties

and organizations and
c) "economic rivalry" antisemitism by merchants. What concerns us here is whether and how any of these types of antisemitism (or a combination of them) found expression in state policy and grass roots attitudes.

There is little evidence of public manifestations of religious antisemitism in the interwar period. Commercial rivalry among Greeks and Jews in Thessaloniki is bound to have existed. It is not clear whether it was actually exacerbated or eased by the decline in Jewish business following the city's transformation from an erstwhile Ottoman commercial center into a northern Greek outpost. In any case, this cause of hostility must have fueled part of the instances of popular antisemitism witnessed in Thessaloniki. But hostility on a political level seems to have been more important. In what can be considered the definitive study on Greek interwar (1922-1933) politics,[15] Mavrogordatos has described the policy of the ruling Venizelist party as being one of hellenization of the recently-acquired areas in northern Greece which contained a number of different ethnic minorities. A number of measures were taken by the state which adversely affected the Jews such as making Sunday an obligatory holiday and setting up a separate Jewish (and Muslim) electoral college, although the Jews were not the only minority to be affected by the Venizelist measures. As a result of these policies the Jews and other minorities in northern Greece voted consistently for the anti-Venizelist politic bloc. In fact the Zionist movement, which had developed earlier in Thessaloniki, was explicitly directed against the incorporation of the Jews into Greek society. The socialist movement, which was particularly strong among the Jews, had its own reasons for opposing Greek nationalism. This left a small minority of the community, the "moderates" supporting assimilation. The fear of what Mavrogordatos calls "the alien as arbiter" in marginal electoral areas led Venizelist politicians and journalists to conjure up images of the Jews colored by antisemitism. In doing so they must shoulder some of the blame for the burning down of the (Jewish) Cambell district in Thessaloniki in 1931 and especially for the antisemitic tension in the city on the occasion of a by-election in 1933. However, Mavrogordatos is careful to distinguish between official Venizelist policy and the utterances of politicians and journalists:

> Neither official Venizelism nor Venizelos personally was ever identified with truly antisemitic attitudes. In fact, they had always reacted strongly against manifestations of antisemitism.[16]

The policy of the state following Thessaloniki's incorporation into Greece bears out Bernard Lewis' assessment that:

> The Jews of Salonika, familiar with the long record of commercial rivalry and antisemitic agitation of their Greek neighbors, viewed this change with considerable misgiving. Their fears about their possible fate under a Greek government proved to be misplaced.[17]

Antisemitism, expressed on a political level by ardent nationalists in interwar Greece seemed to lack overt racist undertones and was certainly not couched in terms claiming any philosophical validity. The antisemitic propaganda of a tiny fascist party was more genuine. The Metaxas dictatorship, however, which ruled from 1936 until the war, was tolerant towards the Jewish community. Although it is difficult to draw up a balance sheet between conscious non-assimilation and antisemitism, there are sufficient indications that the former phenomenon remained important on the eve of Nazi occupation of Greece.

The ethnic, regional, religious and political cleavages of interwar Greece seem to have been put aside after Italy attacked Greece in October 1940. Even the outlawed communists joined the struggle to defend the country against the invaders under the leadership of the dictatorial regime. Under conditions of mass mobilization the regime had to abandon its discriminatory posture. Only political prisoners and Venizelist medium and high-ranking officers (who were out of favor with the regime) were forcibly kept away from the front. After the country's occupation in 1941, the emergence of resistance organizations stressing their national character is revealing enough of the primary feature of Greek wartime society.[18] Political and class conflict which resurfaced soon centered on the most appropriate form of national unity and resistance. Students of this period are well aware of the premium attached to "national unity" by the communists. Under such circumstances one can understand how the Greek Jews were counted on the side of the anti-Axisnational alliance. This process began immediately with the mobilization for the war against the Italians in which a number of Greek Jews distinguished themselves in battle. It remains as yet unknown whether they were from the southern communities or the less assimilated northern communities. Colonel Frizis, whose heroic sacrifice has often been cited in Greek Jewish sources, was of Romaniot origin.

When, later on, Jews were being singled out for discriminatory treatment, the resistance movement did not remain indifferent. It could not be of any practical help in Thessaloniki when the deportations began because the city was then out of reach of the various guerrilla organizations. Nor were they able to do much in the urban centers of the Bulgarian zone. But when measures against the Jews were introduced in what had been the Italian zone up to 1943, the resistance organizations were in a position to be of practical help especially in the Athens area. The policy of a number of Greek organizations and institutions described below, was both supportive and effective. These organizations and institutions, including the Church, the Athens Police and the communists, reflect a broad range of the political spectrum. This confirms the assertion that discrimination was inoperative in the context of "national unity".

The most important of the main resistance organizations was EAM (National Liberation Organization) with its army ELAS. EAM was dominated by the communists. Its political aim was the creation of a front of national unity against the Axis which would fight for liberation; subjects such as the future socialist transformation of the country, were carefully avoided. About 400 Jews joined EAM and became ELAS guerrillas. Several either fell in battle or were caught and executed but the Axis forces as resistance fighters, among them an ELAS colonel named Mordoch. A number of them were honored with posthumous promotion (ELAS did not award medals). A strong Jewish presence in EAM /ELAS comes as no surprise since the Left in Greece had always had Jewish participation. The most important socialist trade union in early 20th century Greece (it joined the Communist Party in 1918) was the Thessaloniki *Federacion Socialista Laboradera,* a majority of whose members were Jews. Abraham Benaroya is considered one of the founders of Greek socialism, while Alberto Curiel was one of the first parliamentary deputies of the Left.[19]

The recently published memoirs of a leading figure of the resistance and ensuing Civil War, Markos Vaphiades, confirm that Thessaloniki's EAM was in close contact with the Jewish community leaders through its own Jewish members. EAM was unable to prevail upon the latter to escape the 1943 roundups because most EAM Jews chose to remain with their families.[20] Being a centralized and efficient organization, EAM was able to inform its Athens section of the Nazi measures in Thessaloniki. Thus, when the Nazis decided to move against the Athens Jews they neither surprised the Jewish leadership nor caught EAM unprepared. The EAM underground press had published regular appeals to the population to assist their Jewish compatriots while the organization had facilitated the passage of Greek Jews to the Middle East as well as recruiting volunteers into its ranks. It is worth recording here excerpts from the EAM Report on the activity of its Jewish sector in Athens, bearing in mind that this was published by EAM after the war:

> It tackled their special problems. It organized the relief of the Jewish refugees from Thessaloniki. Through the efforts of the organization, community kitchens and medical centers were founded and the problems of housing, clothing and employment were solved ...Bread and food rations were issued ...Thus, when the pogrom was delcared, the Sector headed the struggle against the pogrom. It issued the slogan: "No one is to present himself"...The EAM found hundreds of houses for the Jews who had abandoned their own habitations.[21]

The existence of a separate "Jewish Sector" in the Athens EAM did not imply discrimination among members. An important feature of the organization was its formation into separate groups made up of people who came from the same area. This method guaranteed greater security against infiltrator. Several Jews who expressed their concern about the "segregation" were quickly persuaded of its advantages.[22]

EAM's most spectacular feat in Athens when the Nazis began to hunt in earnest for the Jews (after they had taken over the administration of Athens in September 1943 from the Italians), was the escape of the Chief Rabbi Elias Barzalai to the EAM/ELAS controlled mountains. The rabbi had been urged by a number of people to destroy the lists of Jews and go into hiding but it was EAM which presented him with a safe way of doing so. The "Rosenberg Committee" which had arrived from Thessaloniki asked the rabbi for the lists of Jews in the city of Athens. On 22 September 1943 he asked for a few days notice. When they tried to contact him they found out that his house had been "broken into" the lists burned and Barzalai was nowhere to be found. He had been escorted out of Athens by a group of Jewish EAM members, among whom was Baruch Shiby and aided by two leading figures in EAM, Vasandis and Kefalidis. On 14 October 1943 the EAM underground newspaper *Eleftheri Ellada* published the following announcement:

> The Chief Rabbi of Athens Elias Barzalai sends a message to the Greek people in which he begs them to imitate the example of the EAM for the saving of the Greek Israelites against whom the Hitlerite beasts have unleashed their monstrous persecution.[23]

The rabbi traveled to many parts of mountainous "Free Greece" and was received with honors everywhere. Usually, when Barzalai had to make an overnight stay, the local Orthodox priest would insist he lodge with him as a guest.[24]

Meanwhile, in Athens the Nazis were incensed at the rabbi's escape and the disappearance of the lists.

The "Supreme Commander of the Security and Police" issued an order on 3 October 1943 obliging the Athenian Jews to register at the synagogue. A few days later, on October 10, the EAM underground newspaper *Rizospastis* called upon the population to ridicule the Nazi measures and offer asylum to the Jews. What followed has been described by Stavrianos:

> The Christian Greeks responded to these appeals. Only a minority of Athens Jews obeyed the registration order. The remainder fled their habitations and were given shelter by the populace, despite the harsh reprisals inflicted by the Germans when hidden Jews were discovered. Systematic filtering through to Free Greece was then organized. Special EAM cadres were assigned the task. A transport agency was established which made available automobiles, liaison and funds. Whole busloads of refugees started out from Canning Square and other such centers in Athens... A total of 3.000 Athenian Jews were saved in this manner.[25]

Another report, by the World Jewish Congress, includes descriptions of how EAM assisted a number of Jews to travel to Palestine via the Aegean islands and Turkey. According to this second report, priority was given to Jews on the boats and each wealthy Jew being transported was asked to make a contribution covering traveling costs for two fellow Jews. The *Histadrut* (Jewish Federation of Workers in Palestine) sent letters of thanks to EAM as well as material aid.

The largest number of Jews remained hidden in Athens benefiting from the discreet underground presence of EAM in the city. A young Thessaloniki Jew, Mario Modiano, ventured outside his hiding place only once a week in order to exchange sovereigns for cash. On several occasions he was intercepted by EAM members in some districts who were suspicious of his circuitous route. When he told them that he was a Jew in hiding they even offered to escort him to his destination.[26] Towards the end of the war Rabbi Barzalai made a moving public statement thanking EAM for its invaluable help to the Jewish community. EAM, the most powerful and the most effective of all Greek resistance organizations, had the best record in this respect.

The Orthodox Church remained in operation in Athens throughout the occupation and Archbishop Damaskinos played an important role in religious and political affairs during this period. His importance was reflected in his appointment as Regent after Greece's liberation. Damaskinos' biographer mentions that the Archbishop received a number of committees and representatives asking him to intervene on behalf of the Thessaloniki Jews in early 1943.[27] Damaskinos saw the Plenipotentiary for the Reich in Greece and made a strong complaint about the measures being taken against the Jews in Thessaloniki. After the first deportations had begun, the Archbishop organized a meeting of leading academics, judges and lawyers as well as the presidents and secretaries of trade unions and professional associations. A petition to the quisling government was drafted expressing the horror of the Greek people at the deportations and demanding that these should stop immediately:

> The Greek Jews have not only established themselves as valuable contributors to the country's economic life but they have also observed the law and demonstrated that they have understood what their duties are as Greeks. Thus they have participated in the common sacrifices and struggles of the Greek nation to defend its inalienable rights... the Greek Jews are part of the most peaceful, law-abiding and productive people in this land.[28]

The petition to the quisling government was signed by Damaskinos and another 27 public figures. For good measure, a similar one was sent to the Reich's Plenipotentiary. Meanwhile Damaskinos contacted the International Red Cross Representative in Greece and organized relief for the Jews in Thessaloniki. He also transmitted financial aid from Athens Jews to Thessaloniki through the Orthodox Metropolitan there. When the moves against the Athens Jews began, Damaskinos called for the General Director of the Administrative Services of the Athens Municipality and told him that he was going to "baptize them as Christians'. He asked that the General Director issue them with the necessary Municipality certificate that they would also need to acquire identity papers proving them to be Christian Greeks. General Director Chaldezos agreed to Damaskinos' plan and 560 Jews were registered as Christians.[29]

The Chief of the Athens Police during the occupation, Colonel Angelos Evert, was secretly in contact with the British. His position enabled him to make an important contribution to the cause of the resistance. On Evert's orders the police issued about 18.500 false identity papers in order to protect all those hiding from the German authorities including Greek Jews. They were also allowed to hide in police stations for short periods of time and were at times escorted by policemen in order to avoid German security checks.[30] Evert together with three senior police officers (D. Vranopoulos, M. Glykas and D. Vlastaris) were honored by the Yad Vashem Institute in 1970. Evert's son Miltiades recalls a humorous note in the police's effort to releave the Jews. A number of Jews were taken into the police to serve as officers. In order to make things as realistic as possible, many of them were placed on duty at public ceremonies at Orthodox Churches. On a more serious note, the same informant states that the police hid the Aliens register containing the names of Jews, from the Germans. After the war, the police were asked for the register by the British in connection with their policy in Palestine. The police burnt the register and claimed that it had been destroyed during the occupation.[31]

A number of small informal resistance groups operated in Athens during the war years. A member of one of these groups, Constantinos Calligas, has recounted how his group was active in protecting Jewish families in Athens. Calligas was a schoolboy at the time and met several Jewish children at a French school in

Athens. Many families who had fled from Thessaloniki early chose to send their children to schools in Athens which provided a French education. As the moves against the Jews in Athens began, the question of offering them protection was "purely a matter of protecting friends". Those like Calligas who had become involved in clandestine activities were better placed to be of practical help. Safe houses were found and provisions were also procured. This particular group was active in assisting Jews with Spanish nationality who were allowed to leave Athens for Spain in April 1994. Calligas and his companions smuggled various valuables through the German cordon around the synagogue where the departees had assembled to be searched before embarkation.[32]

A great deal of further research would be needed to provide the whole picture of the attitude of the Athenians towards the Jews during the occupation. The examples cited above are not the only ones. Emmanuel Arouch, a member of EAM's Jewish sector who later on fought with ELAS in the mountains, recalls a revealing detail: when Athens was liberated and the Jews emerged from wherever they were hiding, it transpired that the whole neighborhood had been aware of their presence all along.[33] This silent assent on behalf of many Athenians towards protection of Jews against Nazis is a telling indication of the situation in the Greek capital: the broad opposition front against the Nazis did not think twice about including the Greek Jews in its ranks. The case of wartime Athens might be a small chapter in the history of the Gentile attitude towards the European Jews. By virtue of its importance in the salvation of a part of Greek Jewry the implications of what happened there cannot be ignored. The Athenian case contained two determinant factors in Greek attitudes towards the Jews: a degree of assimilation in and acceptance by society and the presence of an effective anti-fascist resistance movement.

NOTES

This chapter was first published in <u>FORUM on the Jewish People, Zionism and Israel</u>, Summer 1987, Issue no. 60.

I am grateful for the help I received during my research from the Jewish Community of Thessaloniki, the Editors of <u>Chronica</u> of the Central Council of Jews in Greece, the Jewish Museum of Greece in Athens and to those whose names appear in the appropriate foot-note. Professor Mavrogordatos comments on an earlier draft were of great benefit to me.

1. John O. Iatrides ed. *Greece in the 1940s A Bibliographic Companion* (University Press of New England, Hanover and London, 1981). Both bibliographies in this volume, by Hagen Fleischer and Steven Bowman are relevant.

2. *Chronica* nos. 53,54,56 and 60. *Chronica* is the monthly publication of the Central Jewish Council of Greece.

3. Joseph Ben, "Jewish Leadership in Greece During the Holocaust" in *Partners of the Jewish Leadership in Nazi Europe* (Yad Vashem, 1977) pp. 335 - 352. Rachel Dalven "The Holocaust in Jannina" in *Journal of Modern Greek Studies* Vol. 2, No. 1, May 1984, pp. 87-103.

4. Yehuda Bauer, *The Holocaust in Historical Perspective* (Seattle, 1978) p. 52.

5. Molho, M. and Nehama J. *In Memoriam, Jewish Community of Thessaloniki, Thessaloniki, 1976, p. 351. There was a 2.200 strong community on the island of Rhodes which was not part of Greece then.

6. A more detailed summary can be found in J. L. Hondros, *Occupation and Resistance: The Greek Agony 1941-44*, Pella Publishing, New York 1983 pp. 90-94.

7. Bauer, *op. cit.* p. 91.

8. Errikos Sevillas, *Athens - Auschwitz*, Translated and Introduced by Nikos Stavroulakis (Lycabettus Press, Athens 1983) p. XIX.

9. Leon Sciaky, *Farewell to Salonika* (Current Books, New York 1946) pp. 115-6.

10. Ben, *op. cit.* pp. 344-52.

11. Dalven, *op. cit.* pp. 101-3.

12. An antisemitic outburst in 1847 after the Greek prime minister had forbidden the burning of a "Judas" during Easter at the request of Max Rothschild. See Stavroulakis, *op. cit.* p. XII.

13. Antisemitism by the Romanian and Bulgarian states did not mean automatic acquiescence to Nazi policy during the war. On this, apart from the standard works on European Jewry, see Michael R. Marrus & Robert O. Paxton, *Vichy France and the Jews* (Basic Books, New York, 1981) Ch. 8 and Hans Joachim Hoppe, "Germany, Bulgaria, Greece: Their Relations and Bulgarian Policy in Occupied Greece" in *Journal of the Hellenic Diaspora* Vol. XI No. 3 Fall 1984.

14. L.S. Stavrianos, "The Jews of Greece" in *Journal of Central European Affairs*, VIII (Oct., 1948) p. 260.

15. Mavrogordatos G. Th., *Stillborn Republic Social Coalitions*

and *Party Strategies in Greece, 1922-1936* (University of California Press, Berkeley and Los Angeles 1983).

16. *Ibid.* p. 258 Venizelos in fact at first adopted an assimilationist policy which was rejected by the majority of the Jewish community.

17. Bernard Lewis, *The Jews of Islam* (Routledge and Kegan Paul, London 1984) p. 180.

18. See Nicholas Svoronos, "Greek History 1940 - 1950: The Main Problems" in Iatrides, ed., *Greece in the 1940s,: A Nation in Crisis* (University Press of New England, Hanover and London, 1981) pp. 1-14.

19. On the *Federacion* see George B. Leontaritis, *To Elliniko Socialistiko Kinima kata ton Proto Pangosmio Polemo* (Exantas, Athens, 1978); Antonis Liakos, *I Socialistiki Ergatiki Omospondia Thessalonikis (Federacion)* (Paratiritis, Thessaloniki 1985); Kostis Moskoff, *Eisagogika stin Istoria tou Kinimatos tis Ergatikis Taxis* (Thessaloniki, 1979).

20. Markos Vaphiadis, *Apomnimonevmata* Vol. 2, Nea Sinora (Athens 1985) p. 87.

21. EAM Central Committee Report "The Jews and the Liberation Struggle" (n.p.n.d.).

22. Personal communication by Emmanuel Arouch, (Aug. 1985).

23. EAM Central Committee Report, *op. cit.*

24. Personal Communication by E. Arouch.

25. EAM Central Committee Report *op. cit.*

26. Personal Communication by Mario Modiano (July 1985). Mr. Modiano is currently the Athens correspondent of the *London Times*.

27. Elias Venezis, *Archiepiscopos Damaskinos*, (Hestia, Athens, 1981) rprnt. p. 261.

28. *Ibid.* pp. 266-68.

29. *Ibid.* p. 269.

30. S. Andonacos "I Astinomia Poleon Arogos ston Agona ton Evreon" in *Chronica* No. 33 Nov. 1980.

31. Personal communication by Miltiades Evert (July 1985). Mr. Evert is currently a member of the Greek Parliament and the President of the New Democracy Party.

32. Personal communication by Constantinos Calligas (June 1985). Mr. Calligas was a columnist in the Athens daily *Kathimerini.*

33. Personal communication by Emmanuel Aruch (Aug. 1985).

DOCUMENTS:

THE JEWS IN GREECE, 1941-1944
EYEWITNESS ACCOUNTS[*]

Introduction

The nearly total extermination of Greece's 80,000-strong Jewish community during the Second World War is broadly known. Specialists of this period are familiar with the more detailed aspects of the Nazi measures designed to apply the "final solution" in Greece, as well as the assistance Greek Jews received from resistance organizations and individuals. A number of monographs addressing specific issues related to the fate of Greek Jewry are beginning to appear.[1] In fact, the quantity of information on Greek Jews during the war, both in terms of empirical data as well as of working hypotheses, is already demanding a more

---

[*] The original phrasing of these texts has been retained. The classification appearing on the top of each document — RESTRICTED, CONFIDENTIAL and SECRET — refers to the three-tiered classification system established by the War Department in 1917; RESTRICTED is the lowest one and SECRET the highest.

The documents which follow were collected with the kind help of Nikos Papaconstantinou in Washington, D.C..

synthetic approach. Such an approach would consist of placing the Jewish question of wartime and prewar Greece in a broad social context rather than isolating its separate aspects for the purpose of analysis. It is toward the formulation of such an approach that the following documents are being published here. These documents consist of accounts of the conditions faced by Jews in wartime Greece related by Jews who managed to leave occupied Greece. These descriptions appear in the documents of four separate sources of information. The first is the U.S. Office of Censorship, which monitored information in the Allied and Axis press; the second is the Military Attaché's office in Istanbul, Turkey; the third is the U.S. Consulate in Istanbul and the fourth is the Office of Strategic Services. It must be stressed that what follows is neither a full set of documents on the Jews in wartime Greece, nor a complete series of documents on this subject by each of the four separate services. It is, rather, a selection of these which reflects the overall picture of the circumstances under which the fate of the Jews tied in with the general situation in wartime Greece.

These descriptions are among the very few contemporary records of how ordinary people experienced the Nazi extermination of Greek Jews. Eyewitness accounts are an area where scholarly research has learned to tread carefully. If we allowed the facts to "speak for themselves", we would be censoring the role of the historian. The value, however, of these documents, beyond their empirical content, is in *how* the interviewees depict the situation they left behind them in Greece.

The picture invariably presented is one of the general conditions of the country, with the personal or collective Jewish aspects woven into a broader canvas. One gets a sense of daily living conditions, Nazi repression, and the response of the resistance movement. This seems a profitable starting-point for a synthetic examination of the Holocaust in Greece.

Most of the reports mentioned above were by Thessaloniki Jews with Turkish citizenship, who were allowed to travel to Turkey. The sources of the rest of the reports, it can be assumed were Greek Jews or non-Jewish Greeks. The information suffers from the inevitable factual of chronological inaccuracies of contemporary observations, which are not serious enough to detract from the value of the accounts. One anonymous source, almost certainly non-Jewish, exaggerates the relations between Greek Jews and the rest of the population before the war, which were not unproblematic in Thessaloniki, the main center of Jewish life in Greece. As far as these relations are concerned, the recently published study by George Mavrogordatos on interwar Greek politics[2] has contributed to a better understanding of them. The antisemitic incidents which did take place in Thessaloniki were connected with the unresolved issue of the unassimilated minorities in northern Greece and their anti-Venizelist electoral behavior. While local Venizelists were connected with these incidents, neither official Venizelism nor Venizelos himself sanctioned them in any way: in fact, they condemned them. The accounts published here reflect the fact that the more assimilated mixed-origin communities of the south, including Athens, were assisted more directly by the Greek population than the self-contained Sephardic communities in Thessaloniki and elsewhere. The conditions under which the Sephardic communities remained less assimilated than the older communities have been analyzed in the short but succinct history of Greek Jews by Nikos Stavroulakis.[3] I have argued that assimilation, alongside a developed resistance movement, were the two most important factors in the survival of the Jews of Athens.[4] In Thessaloniki, on the other hand, the resistance movement was not in a position to be of direct help. What help it was able to offer, according to Markos Vaphiadis's memoirs, was rejected; the EAMist Jews preferred to remain with their families during the roundups.[5] Meanwhile, the special responsibilities of the Jewish leadership in Thessaloniki have been pointed out in a number of studies.[6]

A brief chronology of the Nazi measures against Greek Jews[7] may be a useful companion to the eyewitness accounts which follow: as soon as the Nazis occupied Greece, they suspended all Jewish publications and began publishing the antisemitic Greek-language newspaper *Nea Europi* in Thessaloniki. The fifteen-member Jewish Council of the city was arrested. The following year, in July 1942, forced labor was introduced in the Thessaloniki area, a German-occupied zone, causing many Jews to move away from the city and into the Italian-occupied zones to the south. Between 2,000 and 3,000 Jewish young men were dispatched to other parts of Greece to participate in forced labor. Meanwhile, the Bulgarians, who occupied northeast Greece, began taking antisemitic measures which eventually led to the deportation of the Jews of Thrace to Treblinka.[8] In November 1942, the first confiscations of Jewish property in Thessaloniki occurred. The systematic expropriation and requisitioning of Jewish property began in January. In February, the Nazis issued orders forcing all but foreign Jews to be marked with armbands and yellow stars, and their stores identified as Jewish with appropriate notices. The first deportations began the same month. By August, about 46.000 Thessaloniki Jews had been deported to Auschwitz and Birkenau.

The "final solution" was delayed for the other, smaller, Jewish settlements in Greece because these were within the Italian-occupied zones. The Italians had refused to participate in the Nazi measures. Italy's withdrawal from the Axis in September 1943 meant the beginning of Jewish persecution all over the country, which now came under Nazi occupation. The Athens Jews were ordered to register in October, but very few did so. Aided by EAM, Chief Rabbi Barzalai burned the registers and escaped to the mountains. Jewish property was promptly confiscated in the capital.

In the series of raids in the spring of 1944, about 5.000 Jews were seized and deported in Athens and the rest of the mainland. Relatively few Jews were rounded up in the Volos-Trikala-Larissa area, where EAM-ELAS were powerful, but in the northwestern town of Ioannina almost all of the small community were deported. The same occurred with the small communities on the islands of Rhodes, Corfu and Crete. The 300 or so Jews on the island of Zakinthos were allowed by the Austrian commander there to escape to Italy before the arrival of the SS.

Throughout 1943 and 1944, a number of foreign consulates were successful in rescuing a number of Jews with non-Greek passports. But the largest number of Jews survived within Greece through the protection offered by EAM and a variety of sources, including Archbishop Damaskinos and Chief of Athens Police Angelos Evert, and of course, a large number of the population.

I. Censorship Reports
These are filed under the heading:
Greece: Political and Civil Rights

CONFIDENTIAL

GREEK JEWS SENT TO GHETTO IN GREECE

The German "Donau Zeitung", published in Belgrade, Serbia, reports that all Salonica Jews will be sent to Ghettos on the Island of Crete. They will be compelled to leave all their possessions behind them, as punishment for "making Greece fight the Axis".

Source: Office of Censorship U.S.A. Record No. CH 5674, Sept. 14, 1942.

RESTRICTED

JEWISH POPULATION IN GREECE

International Press Agency, 5.1.43. It is reported from Athens that the number of Jews in Greece totals 100,000 or 1.5% of the population. In Greece proper (Peloponnese and Thessaly) the number of Jews is small. In Athens there are 2,000, on Corfu 3,500 and on Crete 600. The majority of Jews live in southern Macedonia, and out of the total population of 250,000 in Salonica, there are 70,000 Jews. (The 1928 census gave the number of Jews in Greece as 72,791, though a later estimate in 1938 suggested 75,000. According to the 1928 census, 60,484 were in Macedonia, of which 55,983 lived in Salonica and 2,166 in Kavalla-Ed.).

Source: News Digest, No. 1038 (E. H. Series) January 23, 1943).

CONFIDENTIAL

NAZIS IN GREECE PREVENT JEWS FROM SECURING FAIR SHARE OF SHIPMENTS OF FOOD AND MEDICINE

Greek Jews have received very little benefit from the shipments of food and medicine which were sent to Greece with British permission it is reported here this week.

Axis officials throughout the country see to it that

as few supplies as possible are distributed to Jews; in Salonica, for instance, Jews received only five per cent of the share to which they were entitled on the basis of their proportion to the general population.

Source: United States of America National Censorship, Records No. BER 15146/42, April 3, 1942.

{NO CLASSIFICATION}

Some of the Jewish Communities in Greece, like those of Chalcis, Janina, Arta, and Corfu, are very ancient. Their origin is lost in antiquity. For instance, amongst the ruins of Delos, the sacred island of Ancient Greece, reputed to have been the birth place of Apollo and a great centre of worship throughout the pagan ages, the remains of the Synagogue are still to be seen.

The modern Community of Salonica, the largest in Greece, is a settlement of Spanish Jews who fled there from the persecutions of Isabella of Castille and Ferdinand the Catholic. They still speak amongst themselves a Spanish dialect in which many archaic forms of language were preserved, and many of them had Judaeo-Spanish names. Ever since Greece recovered her independence by conquest in 1830, the laws of the Kingdom have granted full civil and social rights to the Jews of Greece. At no time have these rights been denied or questioned, and at no time have the Greek people allowed themselves to be reached by any of the successive waves of anti-Semitism which have periodically swept over Europe; in fact, anti-Semitism is entirely unknown in Greece and entirely alien to the national character. Neither had the Jews, during domestic controversies, some of which have been extremely acute, been made as in so many other countries, scape-goats for public misfortunes. This is all the more remarkable because the Jews in those parts of Greece which were most recently united to the Kingdom (Salonica, for instance), although completely assimilated as far as the national consciousness and the actual participation in the nation's life are concerned (they were always represented in Parliament by Jewish members), have been entirely free to retain their own dialect, a form of Judaeo-Spanish which they speak amongst themselves, and their own customs.

In more recent years the Greek Jews have always shared the vicissitudes of their country of adoption. In the present war against Fascism and Nazism, many Jews have distinguished themselves by their gallantry in military action. A particularly memorable example was given by the Jewish Colonel Frizis, of the Greek Royal Infantry, a member of the very ancient Jewish Community of Chalcis, in Euboea. Colonel Frizis, after a series of feats of arms, were killed on his horse, which he refused to dismount, in total disregard of danger, during an attack by dive-bombers. The Greek Press published a detailed account of this heroic death, together with the letter of condolence addressed to his widow by the late Prime Minister of Greece, in which he informed her that the Colonel's children would be brought up in the nation's care.

Soon after the invasion of Greece, the Gestapo, which arrived on the heels of the German Army, enforced, together with other general measures of oppression and terrorism, the introduction of anti-Jewish measures, forbidding Jews to practice certain professions, to enter cafes, restaurants, theatres, cinemas, etc. The repercussions of such measures were keenly felt in Salonica, where the Jewish Community is very large. These measures, dictated by a hated and despised enemy, and directed against compatriots who had taken a full and honorable part in this last total war of the Greek nation, were met with profound indignation by Greek public opinion, and with such stubborn opposition that their efforts were entirely neutralized. It seems that even the Puppet Government, under authorities had a formal protest against anti-Semitic measures.

Information reaching London from the underground newspaper *E Mahomene Ellas* (Fighting Greece) and from other sources, reveal something of the recent position of Jews in Axis-occupied Greece.

In the month of August, 1942, the German authorities ordered all male Jews between the ages of 16 and 40 to assemble in Salonica, the intention being, apparently, to send them to a specially organized ghetto to be established in Crete. When 9,000 had been rounded up, the Germans paraded them and forced them to march and run for two hours, then beat them indiscriminately. About 100 of the prisoners fell unconscious as a result of this treatment, and two died. Informers who were present pointed out those Jews who were known to have property, and the Germans by means of extreme ill-treatment extorted money and jewelry from them.

A solemn warning was issued by Greek Orthodox Church authorities that if the Germans persisted with a plan to send the Jews to the Crete ghetto, or if they deported them to Poland, there would be a general uprising of the entire population: accordingly the plan was abandoned. Instead, the Jews were sent to a concentration camp in the Macedonian Mountains. Where they were condemned to forced labor, road-building and farm work.

Apparently 8,000 of these Jews reached the concentration camp, for in October, various Greek quisling newspapers reported that of that number some 200 had been fettered and thrown into prison because they attempted to escape and join the guerrillas operating from mountain bases.

Source: Report No. 6, Issued by The Inter-Allied Information Committee, London, May 1943.

CONFIDENTIAL

POLITICAL AND CIVIL RIGHTS

Of the 55,000 Jews in Salonica, only about 5,000 foreign Jews, mostly of Spanish and Turkish nationality remain, all the rest having been deported to Poland. The entire property of the Greek Jews is said to have been confiscated. (J. T. A. 24/27/5/43). There has been no further reference to anti-semitic regulations in central and southern Greece.

Source: Postal and Telegraph Censorship report on Jewry, Period: January to June, 1943. London 9th August 1943.

II. Military Intelligence Division W.D.G.S
Reports by the Military Attaché in Istanbul

Report No. 12
July 17, 1943
Source and degree of reliability: B-2, Turkish subject.

The following statement was made by Jaco Menashe, Turkish subject, on July 14, 1943. The statement is self-explanatory. Mr. Menashe has resided in Salonica, Greece, for many years.

"Some 10 days ago I was called by the Turkish Consul, who came to Salonica from Athens and informed that I and some 8 or 10 Turkish subject Jews must leave immediately for Turkey, otherwise we would be sent out of the country with other Greek Jews. Finally, the Consul was able to persuade the Germans to give us a few extra days and with several others I left Salonica Thursday morning, the 8th of July, and arrived in Istanbul Monday, the 12th of July.

We changed trains at Cevgeli, Iskub, Sofia and Buleburgas.

With the exception of about 100, all the Greek Jews of Salonica have been deported in the direction of Niche but to what destination is not known. This mass deportation started about the 27th of March and lasted about one month and a half. Deportees were allowed to take practically nothing with them. They were packed into closed wagons, many wagons used for transportation of cattle, etc. The men and women were separated, children up to 7 years were allowed with their mothers. Over 7 years were separated male and female. I know one woman who was sent who had had a child the day before.

The 100 still left in the Ghetto (the poor district known as the Baron Hirsch) consist of the Hebambashi, several of his assistants, secretaries and so forth and it is said that as soon as Jews, who have been used in Thrace in labor corps, return to Salonica, they will make up a large convoy and they will all be sent. The laborers are now being called in. Italian, Turkish and Spanish Jews have not been sent. No news or letters have been received from any of the deportees. One man whom I know, a certain Hasson, was brought back to Salonica, imprisoned and beaten up for several days until he finally confessed that he had handed over to a certain Valera, druggist, 700 gold liras for safekeeping before he left. He was then taken into custody by two German officers who brought him back to Salonica, together with the Jew who had given him away, and then went to Valera who was forced to admit having the gold. This was handed over and was divided equally between the German officers and the Jew. Hasson was then deported to follow the others.

Between Salonica and Niche I saw 7-8 trains daily of 30-40 wagons, some of them with two locomotives, filled with German and Austrian troops moving slowly towards Salonica. I saw a certain number of Bulgarians on these trains but did not see any train entirely made up of Bulgarians. I saw some 8-10 trucks with tanks, some of them with one and some with two tanks. Nearly all the Germans on these trains appeared to be young boys from 16 to 18 years of age. During the last few weeks I saw a number of Bulgarian troops arrive in Salonica and the next day saw quite a few of these same Bulgarians changed into German uniforms. After Pantelleria a certain number of German troops left Salonica moving northwards and there was a rumor that those were being sent to Avlona.

From a Greek who arrived from Athens shortly before I left and who was on his way to Germany, I was informed (and this information was confirmed by other sources) that within the last three or four weeks four bridges and a tunnel on the Athens-Salonica line had been blown up by Greek bands, the bridges between Larrissa and Athens and the tunnel west of and not very far from Larrissa. One Greek stated that it will not be possible to repair the line before the end of August. The line is very little used for passenger traffic and military traffic-have to change trains at the blown up sections.

I was informed that the Platamona bridge was blown

up by Greek bands on June 28-30. Till a month ago, 500-600 Italians were stationed at Salonica. Recently these have been considerably increased, maybe up to 5,000-6,000 all coming from Athens. Many Greek police and gendarmes have been brought into Salonica and have been replaced in Thrace by Bulgarians, who have now occupied towns and villages in considerably increased numbers. Many Greek civilian refugees have come in to Salonica from Thrace increasing the already swollen population to 900,000 against a peace-time population of 450,000.

It was rumored that Bulgarians [sic] troops would come in to Salonica. This created a panic, food prices rose to new heights and many articles of food disappeared from the market, but the Bulgarians eventually reached a place some 20 kilometers outside of Salonica and up to the time I left there were no unusual additions to the comparatively few Bulgarian soldiers ordinarily seen in the streets.

I saw no troop movements between Niche and Sofia either way, from Plovidiv to the Turkish frontier all blinds were drawn and I was unable to see any movements."

> Cedric H. Seger
> Captain, A.C.,
> Assistant Military Attaché.
> Forwarded:
> Richard G. Tindall,
> Brigadier General,
> U.S.A. Military Attaché.

RESTRICTED

Report No. 82666
4 November 1943

PROCLAMATION TO THE JEWS OF ATHENS

Source and degree of reliability: Jewish Agency Representative. B-2.

All Jews who come under the jurisdiction of the German administration must remain in the places of residence where they were before 1.6.1943. Jews are forbidden to leave or exchange residences. Jews who are now in Athens and vicinity must report themselves within 5 days at the Jewish Community Center of Athens, and write their names in the lists there. At that time they must give their addresses. In regions outside Athens these duties must be fulfilled at competent municipal or community offices. Jews who do not obey this order will be shot immediately. Non-Jews, who shelter Jews or help them to escape will be immediately sent to concentration camp or given a more severe punishment.

Jews of foreign nationality must appear at the Community Center at Athens at 8 a.m., on 18.10.43 and show their identity papers. Outside Athens this inspection will be by the above mentioned competent authorities.

The Jewish Community of Athens is named the sole agent for all Jewish affairs in Greece, nomination to take effect immediately.

The Jewish Community shall immediately choose a senior Counsellor, who will take over this duty forthwith...

CONFIDENTIAL

Report No. 221
November 20, 1943

1. Istanbul Report No. 221, Nov. 20, 1943.

2. Comment by. C. Lagoudakis: What is said about the Jews in Greece in this report is confirmed from other sources. The sympathy of the Greeks toward their Jewish fellow citizens is a useful story. Position of Jews in Athens.

Greece

Committee of Greek Refugees in Istanbul Protect Identity of Source.

The following statement of the position of Jews in Athens is the most detailed which has yet come to our hands.

When the Jews were expelled form Salonica, about three thousand of them made their way to Athens in a sad plight, no ration cards, etc. This migration raised the Jewish population to about 7,000.

The German Military Governor ordered Athens' Jews to report between the 5th and 10th of October (Piraeus

Jews included, of course) for registration. Jews not Greeks [sic] subjects were given until October 18. Meantime all Jews were to keep off the streets from 5:00 p.m. to 7:00 a.m. and forbidden to change their place of domicile from that of June first.

Each Jew got a white identity card: Jews married to Christians got brown cards — the same distinction having been made at Salonica where several families in which the mother was Christian are still allowed to reside.

All Greeks are explicitly and severely forbidden to give any aid to the Jews. None the less, when the special committee readied itself to indent the registered Jews, scarcely more than a hundred were to be found, the others having been concealed by Greek friends or else taken to the mountains to join the guerrillas.

Executions of Greeks for sheltering Jews are to be expected.

Lewis V. Thomas

III. The Foreign Service
of the United States of America
Correspondence from the American
Consulate-General in Istanbul, Turkey
to the Secretary of State, Washington

Report No. 1083 (R-992)
August 7, 1943

RESTRICTED

SUBJECT: Interview with a Young Jewess who left Salonica July 8, 1943.

SIR:

I have the honor to report an interview with a young Jewess of Turkish nationality, who left Salonica on July 8th and arrived in Istanbul July 15th. This young woman has requested that her name be kept secret. Her report is concerned chiefly with the period March 1st to July 8th and is limited to her personal experience and observations. Since, during the above-mentioned period, she was subjected to the anguish of seeing her husband and friends deported, her interest in matters of a less personal nature was not great. However certain matters of general interest did come to her attention, and while many details of her account have already reached this office through other channels, there remain certain items which are reported herewith. The account includes a description of mass deportations of Greek Jews as carried out by German S.S. troops, a statement of the number of Greek Jews deported, the measures taken with Jews of foreign nationality, an account of food conditions in Salonica and the work of the International Red Cross, a number of items of possible military interest, a statement regarding German morals, and observations upon the journey from Salonica to Istanbul.

Regarding the mass deportation of Jews of Greek citizenship, the young woman reported that the German troops detailed to carry out this work were not the troops already in Salonica but were units of S.S. troops sent especially for the purpose. These troops arrived in Salonica the end of February. Their attitude toward the Greeks, and particularly toward the Jews, was extremely harsh and a distinct contrast to the relatively benevolent attitude of the regular forces of occupation.

The procedure of deportation was as follows: Every Jew was given a form upon which he was ordered to write a complete inventory of his possessions, stating the value of all objects listed and including items which would ordinarily be considered as of no value — such as pet dogs. The next day, these lists had to be turned in, although the interval of less than 24 hours was in many cases not adequate for collecting all the information required. According to our informant, the Jews could see no reason for the inventories, since the S.S. troops paid no attention to those that were submitted, but instead seized every bit of property of all Greek Jews regardless of value. Houses were emptied, the contents carried away in trucks, and the owners were taken to the concentration camp at Baron Hirsch. Articles of value were sent to Germany, while a collection of worthless objects was stored in warehouses.

The wholesale transfer of Greek Jews to the concentration camps began March 2nd and continued for about a month and a half. The concentration camp was completely isolated from the rest of the city. To ensure that there should be no communication between the inmates and the Jews who were still at large, a zone 50 metres wide was established around the camp, which no Jews, whether Greek or of foreign citizenship, could enter upon any pretext whatsoever. Jews who had been living within this area were forced to leave their houses, together with all their possessions, and seek shelter elsewhere. To reinforce the guard of that section of the city, the S.S. troops appointed an auxiliary group of 200 Jewish police. One of these was shot on the spot by an S.S. trooper because he was seen to reply to a question asked by a member of the International Red Cross.

All Greek Jews were taken to the camp, whole families being carried off, regardless of age, sex or physical condition. Inmates of insane asylums and patients from hospitals, including incurable cases, and people suffering from infectious diseases were herded in with the others. All these unfortunate victims were confined for periods of varying length, while they were questioned regarding their property. In case the desired or expected information was not immediately forthcoming, the person questioned was subjected to various forms of torture. The German guards resorted to any expedient which they thought would produce confessions, but a favorite method of persuasion was the burning of finger tips, the procedure being repeated with increasing effectiveness upon each successive application. After this interval of examination, the Jews were sent off in cattle cars, almost without ventilation, 70 to a car. It was believed that their destination was Poland. Forty-five thousand Greek Jews were deported this way.

This figure of 45,000 represents the entire Jewish population of Greek nationality at the time of the deportations. The decrease from the usually accepted estimate of 60,000 was due to the fact that from the time of the German occupation the death rate among the Jews was extremely high — higher than that of the rest of the city —, that many individuals had succeeded in escaping, and also because, beginning with July 1942, groups were sent away almost daily by the occupation authorities to forced labor in Macedonia.

When our informant left Salonica on July 8th, she felt certain that no Jews of any nationality were left in the city. The foreign Jews, numbering about 1000, had been sent according to their nationality to various countries, as listed below:

American Jews to Germany
English Jews to Germany
French Jews to Poland
Italian Jews to Athens
Persian Jews to Germany
Spanish Jews to Spain
Swiss Jews to Switzerland
Turkish Jews to Turkey

This list is almost certainly not complete.

When questioned about food conditions in Salonica previous to her departure, our informant reported that for about a year there had been no lack of food in Salonica if one had the money to pay for it. Though the young woman left Salonica less than a month ago, she herself showed no sign of starvation, but she explained that since the birth of her child nine months ago she had received special food from the International Red Cross. All nursing mothers and children up to twelve years are provided with powdered milk, semolina and sugar. Bread is the only article which is regularly available to everyone through ration cards. A certain amount of white bread is supplied by the International Red Cross at a price of Drs. 600 the oke. White bread is also available on the black market at Drs. 2300 the oke — a fact which immediately causes one to wonder by what channels white flour reaches the black market. The distribution of food supplies by the International Red Cross was described by this young woman as extremely satisfactory.

The interview supplied the following information of possible military importance. The German Commandatur is in the Valeyannis School on the 4th of August Street, opposite the Café Astoria B. During April and May many reinforcements of German troops arrived in Salonica. Our informant said that one was always aware of movements of troops in the city, and the general impression was that considerable forces were continually sent south, but she could not say definitely that there were increased movements at the time of the invasion of Sicily. Parks and streets shaded by trees were full of tanks and military vehicles. Trucks were parked in the Municipal Fair grounds. Communications with Athens were constantly interrupted. In addition to the destruction of the Papadea bridge, there was scarcely a day that the guerrillas were not reported to have caused some damage to the railroad — damage which, however slight, usually necessitated the transfer of freight and passengers by bus at several points on the line. Regarding the air raid over the Sedes airport our informant had heard that there were 600 victims, of whom at least 200 were German killed and wounded. During this raid the Greeks, in their enthusiasm for the Allies, refused to go to their shelters and as a punishment for this the curfew was advanced to 9 p.m. After the Sedes raid the Germans sounded no alert although there were several occasions when bombs were dropped. The young woman reported very few boats in the harbor of Salonica.

German morale in Salonica was low, and suicides were frequent. Typhus is prevalent in the city, but there are not many cases among the Germans. German soldiers are still wearing, as part of their summer uniform, articles of British origin, such as English shorts, shirts, etc.

The departure of the young Jewess from Salonica was arranged by the Turkish consul. She left by train July 8th and changed trains at Gevgeli, where she spent the night. She continued by the usual route, passing through Skopje, Nish, and spending the nights of July 11th and 12th in Sofia. During one of the nights in Sofia there was an air raid alarm which lasted from midnight to 4 a.m.. Between Gevgeli and Skopje our informant saw five or six trains of German soldiers, going south. From Gevgeli on she saw Bulgarian forces of occupation at fairly frequent intervals. While in Sofia she heard for the first time that Bulgarians would occupy Salonica.

> Respectfully yours,
> Burton Y. Berry
> American Consul General

CONFIDENTIAL

Report No. 1327 (R-1228)
September 11, 1943

SUBJECT: Report of an Interview with a Resident of Athens who left that city on August 27.

SIR:

I have the honor to submit a report of an interview with a Syrian Jew of French citizenship, employed for twenty years by an American company in Athens, who has requested that his name be withheld because his family is still in Greece.

The report is introduced by a short account of the trip from Athens and includes information and comments on the following: railway service between Athens and Salonica; the treatment of Jews in Italian-occupied territory; morale of Germans and Italians; troop movements and increase of German control; attitude of the people to the Rallis Government; living conditions with emphasis on price and availability of food; description of the present-day rich; information concerning the oil situation; Greek morale; attitude of the people to the King.

My informant left Athens on August 27 and arrived in Istanbul on September 1. He traveled to Sofia in a plane in which the other passengers were twenty-two German officers. A very short stop at the Sedes airfield near Salonica gave him an opportunity to note that one hangar was completely destroyed and two badly damaged, and that no attempt had been made to remove the debris or to make repairs. It is assumed that the damage was sustained in the raid of June. From Sofia he traveled by rail to Istanbul. Since his permission to leave Greece was granted by the Italian authorities he feared that the Germans might make difficulties either at the Tatoi airfield from which he left or at the Sedes airfield, but although he was questioned briefly, he experienced no trouble.

My informant stated that after his exit permission was given, he waited several weeks for a place on a plane. Asked why, in view of the delay and his urgent desire to leave, he did not travel by rail, he replied that the rail trip was dangerous because of guerrilla activities, and also very long. He stated that it took from four to six days to go from Athens to Salonica. The trains are very slow and great delays result from destruction of bridges, and the consequent necessity of making connections via long detours in trucks or buses. The most serious interruption on the railway line is occasioned by the destruction of a long bridge south of Lamia, presumably the Papadia bridge. My informant did not know at exactly what point one is obliged to leave the railroad south of the bridge, but he had often heard it said that the railway service is resumed at Lianokladi, which is the station of Volo. If this is correct, it would seem to indicate that the railway line is also broken between the bridge and Lianokladi, as the distance is considerable. He had heard that the line was broken at several points between Lamia and Salonica, but he could furnish no details.

My informant said he decided to leave Greece because of the fear that the Germans might take complete control of the Athens region, and begin their customary persecution of the Jews. To date, Jews in Italian-occupied Greece have not been troubled or discriminated against in any way. In fact, Italian occupation authorities are said to have assisted Jews in many ways. For example, my informant estimates that between four and five thousand Jews escaped from Salonica before the deportations, and entered Italian-occupied territory with Italian acquiescence. Although a large proportion probably remained in Athens, many went to join the Jewish colonies in Corfu and Jannina. Examples of assistance given to Jews by individual Italian officials were cited.

My informant made various comments on the morale of the Germans and the relations between Germans and Italians. During the two years of the occupation he had never seen a German and an Italian together. About six months ago people began to notice that Germans occasionally failed to accompany the military salute with the greeting "Heil Hitler", and now it has disappeared entirely. For some weeks the evacuation of German and Italian civilians had been going on, and it is doubtful whether any women or children remain. My informant's wife overheard a wife of a German merchant saying that she had been ordered to leave, and that Vienna had been recommended. She said she could not go to Vienna because she could not find room there, and since she did not want to risk death from bombs in Germany, she had decided to go to Sofia.

Asked about the replacement of Italians by Germans and about troop movements, my informant stated that there had been almost continual movements of both German and Italian troops since the fall of Mussolini, but it was impossible for the ordinary observer to figure out the purpose of them. He believed that German troops in considerable numbers had gone though the city and he had heard that they were headed for the Peloponnesus. There were many more Germans on the streets than formerly, and it seemed certain that their number had greatly increased. He thought that the administration of the city, though still officially Italian, was in reality largely German. On the other hand, Italian policies still prevailed in many quarters, for example the treatment of the Jews. Italians were less in evidence than beforehand, but this was due in part, at least, to the fact that they were ashamed or afraid of making themselves conspicuous. Considering the size of the Italian forces, they had always been less in evidence than one would have expected since, unlike the Germans who requisitioned the hotels and frequented restaurants, they had their own canteens and were quartered some distance from the center of the city in their own establishments. After the fall of Mussolini the Germans had taken measures to prevent Italians from escaping. My informant could not say, however, whether Italians had been withdrawn from Athens or had gone through the city from points south.

My informant confirmed previous reports of complete lack of faith of the people in the Rallis Government. He said that the appointment of Rallis had raised great hopes, for it was generally understood that he had accepted the premiership on definite conditions, two of which were that the Bulgarians should be withdrawn from Greek soil and that the Jews would not be deported. The fact that Rallis immediately went by plane to Salonica increased their hopes, but events soon showed that he was powerless to do anything, and people realized that they could hope for no more from him than from his predecessors...

[There follow two pages with descriptions of poor living conditions and the high morale of the population.]

...Asked to what extent the Greeks were organized secretly for sabotage or for political propaganda, my informant stated that he had heard that such organizations existed, but he knew the name of only one, E.A.M. He had heard Greek friends express opposition to the return of the King but as he was not in touch with political affairs, he could not give definite information as to the extent of this feeling.

Respectfully yours,
Burton Y. Berry
American Consul General

CONFIDENTIAL

Report No. 1746 (R-1616)
November 11, 1943

SUBJECT: Information concerning Jews in Greece

SIR: I have the honor to submit information concerning the fate of Jews deported from Salonica and concerning the situation of Jews in former Italian - occupied territory, and particularly in Athens, since the Germans on October 3 ordered them to register. The information was furnished by the local representative of a Jewish organization.

I. The representative of the Jewish organization made the following statement in an interview:

Of the 50,000 Jews deported from Salonica only about 10,000 reached Poland alive. Included among the dead was the Chief Rabbi of Salonica, 3,000 Jews had previously escaped from Salonica to the Italian - occupied parts of Greece, chiefly to Athens, from which many later went to other places. Jews of Salonica mobilized in

Greece for forced labor, beginning from July 1942 up to the time of the mass deportations in the spring of 1943, are still in Greece. Since these labor battalions are moved from place to place for the building of roads and fortifications, it is difficult to communicate with them. Definite information on how many survive and how they are treated is therefore unavailable. There are reports that they are given light soup three times a day and a kilo of bread each week and that those who become too weak to work are killed. Even so the treatment of those in labor battalions is considered better than those sent to Poland, and this is attributed to the fact that they are serving a useful purpose. Of the 3,500 Jews of Athens probably not more than 600 remain there. The others escaped from the city within fifteen days after the Germans ordered them to register.

II. The German order requiring Jews to register referred to above and reported in Despatch No. 1601 (R-1483) of October 22, 1943, is given below in order to facilitate reference to it.

Regulation

1) All Jews subject to this order must immediately betake themselves to their permanent homes, in which they were living on June 1, 1943.

2) Jews are forbidden to leave their permanent residence or to change their place of residence.

3) Jews in Athens and its environs are obliged to appear within five days at the Jewish Religious Center

in Athens for registration. Those living outside Athens will report to the Greek mayor or to community officers.

4) Jews who do not observe these orders will be shot. Non-Jews who hide Jews, give them shelter or help them to escape, will be sent to labor camps or receive a more severe punishment.

5) Jews of foreign citizenship must report on October 18, 1943, at 8:00 a.m. to the Jewish Religious Center in Athens and there register a copy of their evidence of foreign citizenship. Outside Athens they are to report to the above-mentioned Greek authorities.

6) The Jewish Religious Center in Athens is designated, as from this moment, the only representative of all Jewish interests in Greece. It must immediately form a council of elders and take up its duties. Further instructions will be given later.

7) After registration every male Jew, fourteen years of age and over, must report every second day at the above-mentioned place.

8) Jews are forbidden to walk on the streets or in open places between the hours of 5 p.m. and 7 a.m.

9) The Greek Police will be ordered to control the enforcement of the above order most severely, and immediately to arrest Jews or other persons who prevent its being executed.

10) All those are considered as Jews who have at

least three grandparents of Jewish race, regardless of their religious affiliations.

Athens, October 2, 1943

> The Higher S.S.
> and Police Leader of Greece
> Stroop
> S.S. Brigade Leader and
> General Major of the Police

III. The following is a translation of a written report furnished by the representative of the Jewish organization:

"After the German announcement (requiring Jews to register) every Jew who had provided himself with a card of identity bearing an Orthodox name, was assured a hiding place with Orthodox friends. One must confess that the Athenians have shown a more humane attitude than the people of Salonica and because of that, there is reason to hope that a large part of the Jews can be saved from falling into German hands. There have been cases, however, in which in order to find a safe refuge, it was necessary to pay 1,500,000 to 2,000,000 drachmas monthly or deposit 50 or even 100 gold pounds to the person who gave him shelter as compensation in case the Germans sent him to a concentration camp.

The E.A.M. organization has recruited a large number of our people (Jews) who know English and has sent them to their headquarters. Others, most of them young men, have gone into the mountains to join the guerrillas or to live in the regions known as "Free Greece". The majority have gone to the Karpenisi region and others to Euboea in order to escape by boat. The E.A.M., which has organized several groups, asked everyone in good circumstances to assure the support of two destitute Jews. The organization had distributed leaflets to the Athenians asking them to give assistance. The following is an example of the helpful attitude of the Greeks. At our place of embarkation in Euboea the guerrillas have permitted only Jews to depart and it was only after taking an oath (that they were Jews) that the refugees were allowed to continue their journey.

It is said that during the five-day period specified in the German order only fifty or sixty persons, chiefly those who found no place of refuge, registered. In view of this the Germans prolonged the registration period to October 17 but there were some who registered on October 18 without being penalized. The Germans gave to each one who registered a white card without photographs on which were written the name, address and occupation together with a list of dates, indicating that the bearer should report every second day.

In the case of an invalid an exception was made and he was told to register every fourth day. Those married to Greeks received brown cards. Since the Athenians have shown hostility to the anti-Jewish measures, it is thought that the Germans will be less severe at the beginning in order to bring out those who are hiding. Up to October 20 they had not pillaged any

Jewish shops with the exception of Alhadeff (against whom action was taken as soon as the Italian gave up authority) and that of Eliezer Salomon and a warehouse at 60 Kypseli Street. The furniture of several private houses has been removed, for example Salomon Camhi, Joseph Danon, Sariano, Benzonane, Asseo. Houses of Jews occupied by Greek friends, who have declared that they have bought the property, have not been touched. The hidden Jews will suffer only if the Germans offer rewards to those who denounce them — as such a reward is a great temptation to people suffering from hunger.

The Greek Archbishop has ordered priests to urge in their churches that the Jews be aided. He also intervened with the German authorities to exempt children under 14 and those married to a person of Orthodox faith, and it appears that he was successful. In spite of that it is my opinion that the one hope for the Jews is to escape, for in the long run it is possible that fear of reprisals might influence our Greek friends to change their attitude. With this end in view, it is necessary to confer with several of our sympathizers. I mention the lawyer Andreas Aspealopoulos [*surname unclear on original*] a very good friend of Peppo Benusiglio and Boher Jessurum.

The committee which was formed by the Germans to represent the community is composed of Sciaky and Hadjopoulos and another whose name has not been reported. As you know, the Rabbi Barzilai escaped to the mountains as soon as he was asked for a list of 25 leading Jews. He burned all his records.

I have learned that Athanati has been given the first shipment of 100 pounds sterling but not the second. I advise making future shipments of funds for expenses on land through reputable Greek friends who will get in touch with our people who are subjects of neutral countries. Although these Jews have more liberty of action they are afraid to take the initiative.

Respectfully yours,
Burton Y. Berry
American Consul General

IV. Office of Strategic Services
Reports on Greece

Report No. 10792
Prior to November 16, 1943

SUBJECT: Military and political affairs

All the Jews who were still in Salonica — most of them working in the port and at the station, and living in labor camps without any contact with the population, have been sent away from Salonica, probably to Poland. Jews from Volos and Athens, who were concentrated at a camp at Asvestochori, a few miles from Salonica, have also been sent toward central Europe. All the property of the Jewish community of Salonica is managed by the Bank of Salonica, formerly a Jewish bank but taken over by the Germans since 1941 and now subordinate to the Reichsbank.

New military zones have been created everywhere. The whole of Nikis Avenue, leading from the Customs to the White Tower along the quays, has been prohibited to public traffic. The same applies to all the coastal zone from the Villa Alatini to Kara-Bournou. Part of Tsimiski Street — at the crossing of Venizelos Street has also been declard a military zone.

Great military activity is observable in Salonica. There is a continual travel by plane, of high-ranking German officers between Salonica and Berlin and between Salonica and Sofia.

A few villages on the outskirts of Salonica have been evacuated. Their population has been directed toward Western Macedonia and Thessaly and strictly forbidden to return to Salonica or Volos. Nevertheless, a few peasants and a priest managed to reach Salonica and reported that important Bulgarian forces were advancing toward Salonica. This created panic among the Salonicians which was justified a few days after when three to four thousand Bulgarian soldiers, mostly belonging to the infantry, crossed the city in a southerly direction. However, the evacuation of the neighboring villages had no connection with this movement of Bulgarian troops. The Germans had evacuated the villages for reasons of military safety and in order to install their radio service and a few anti-aircraft units to defend Sedes airdrome.

Another reason for this evacuation is that the Germans, for some time past, have been taking measures for the defense of Salonica from an attack coming from the interior. Such an attack might come either from Greek and Yugoslav patriots or from the Allies, in the event of their landing south of the city and advancing on it from the rear.

Through the press and through all means of propaganda at their disposal, the Nazis have launched a large-scale campaign to pacify Salonician public opinion. They claim there will be no eventual occupation of this city by the Bulgars. They even go as far as to state that in the event of a landing, the Germans alone will take charge of the defense of the city and not a single Bulgar will enter it.

Report No. 11214
End of October 1943

SUBJECT: Anti-semitic measures

Source: Believed reliable

The chief of Security and Police in Greece, Stroop, issued the following decree on October 3, 1943 which concerned the Jews in Athens and neighborhood.

"All Jews under German jurisdiction, i. e. Jews who were Greek subjects, must remain in the place of residence occupied by them before June 1, 1943. Jews are forbidden to leave or exchange their domicile.

"Jews in Athens or vicinity must report in person within five days to the Jewish Community Center in

Athens and register their names and addresses in the lists available for this purpose. In areas outside the precincts of Athens, this registration must be carried out at the municipal or community offices chosen for the purpose. Jews disobeying these orders will be shot immediately, and non-Jews sheltering or helping Jews to escape will immediately be sent to concentration camps or punished more severely.

"Jews of foreign nationality must appear at the Community Center in Athens at 8 a.m.on October 15 to show their identity papers. Outside Athens this inspection of papers will be carried out by the competent municipal or community authorities.

"The Jewish Community Center of Athens has been designated as the sole authority for all Jewish affairs in Greece, this designation to take effect as from the date of publication of this decree. The Jewish Community must choose immediately a senior Counselor who will be the head of the Jewish Community Center in Athens and who will take over his duties forthwith.

"Further instructions will be published from time to time.

"After registration of their names, all male Jews over 14 must report daily at the municipal or community centers.

"No Jews are allowed out between 5 p.m. and 7 a.m.."

Report No. 11205
Early October

SUBJECT: German Measures Against Jews.

Source: Reliable

The persecution of the Jews, which during the Italian occupation had been avoided, has now started for good. Terrified, the Jews seek refuge and safety anywhere and are being led by the Chief Rabbi who disappeared some days ago with the catalogue of all Jews in Athens.

Among others, the following orders were issued by the Germans regarding the Jews:

Jews are not allowed to change or leave their residence. Any Jew not complying with the order regarding registration will be shot. Anyone assisting Jews in any way will be sent to concentration camps. Sheltering Jews is strictly forbidden, and contravention of this order means a heavier penalty being inflicted.

Jews over 14 years old, are obliged to report daily to their registration offices.

Jews are not allowed to cross main streets and squares between 17.00-07.00 hours.

Both the Archbishop and the Government are intervening, but it is expected that their efforts will be fruitless. The Government also sent a memorandum to the German authorities regarding the Jews in Greece, extracts of which are the following:

Jews have become one with the Greek people. They have produced many poets and have repeatedly distinguished themselves on the held of battle.

They have distinguished themselves in military and judicial matters, and have handled delicate matters most conscientiously.

Greek history ignores anti-Semitism and intends doing so now.

The Greek Orthodox Church has always given protection to the Jewish minority, which is small in numbers and offers no racial or political obstacle.

The nature of the Greek people refuses to distinguish people by their races, and judges them only as individuals according to the teachings of the ancient and modern Greek intellectual world.

The enforcement of anti-Semitic measures in Greece would be contrary to the religious feelings of the people, and only very slight protective action is advocated if total repeal is impossible.

CONFIDENTIAL

Report No. 11215
Prior to November 11, 1943

SUBJECT: Anti-Semitic Measures

Source: Unstated

After publication by the Germans of the anti-Semitic decree in Athens every Jew who had previously obtained an identity card with an Orthodox name was able to find a hiding place among Orthodox friends. The Athenian population has displayed far greater humanitarian qualities than the population of Salonica, which gives reason to hope that a large part of the Jews of Athens will be saved from German persecution. There have been cases where one and a half million to two million drachmas have been paid per month for hiding places, and in other cases, deposits of 50 or even 100 gold pounds have been asked for by those offering hide-outs as eventual damages for punishment at the hands of the Germans.

The E.A.M. organization has recruited among the Jews a large number of those who could speak English and has sent them to its headquarters. Others have taken to the mountains, especially the younger ones, and have joined with the partisans, or are living in regions which are known as Free Greece, but the majority have taken shelter in the mountainous regions of Karpenisi and Euboea with the object of ultimately leaving Greece clandestinely by sea.

The EAM, which has organized several convoys, has asked the rich Jews to undertake to keep their less fortunate co-religionists. This organization has also distributed tracks to the Athenian population, asking them to aid and assist the Jews. On one occasion the partisans allowed only Jews to embark on a convoy.

After the publication of the German decree, only 50 to 60 Jews registered, and this was due to the fact that they were unable to find suitable hiding places. The Germans tacitly prolonged the delay for registration to October 17, but no action was taken against certain Jews who registered on the 18th of the month. Those who registered were given white identity cards without photographs, bearing the name, address and profession of the holder, and the dates (every two days) on which he must present himself to the German authorities.

As the population of Athens is showing itself hostile to these measures, it is thought that the Germans will be less severe in the beginning in order to influence those in hiding to register. Up to Wednesday, October 20, 1943, no Jewish shop had been pillaged, with the exception of Aldhadeff, and another belonging to a Jew named Eliazer Solomon. The houses, however, of well-known Jews, were stripped of their furniture. Jews who installed Greek friends in their houses and gave out that they had sold them to these friends have not had them touched by the Germans.

It is probable that Jews who are now in hiding will only risk exposure if the Germans offer large rewards for their denunciation, which rewards will tempt people as a result of famine.

The Greek Archbishop has urged priests to preach assistance to the Jews in their churches. He has also successfully intervened with the German authorities to exempt from racial measures children up to 14 years old and such Jews as are married to persons of Orthodox faith.

CONFIDENTIAL

Report No. 13270
Prior to December 7, 1943

SUBJECT: Anti-semitic measures.

Source: Greek Jew of Salonica, left Athens December 7, 1943.

Athens

While Athens was under control of the Italians, the Italians agreed with the Germans that restrictions should be put on Jews, but this was only a written agreement and never put into effect. In fact, they protected the Jews against the Germans. With their departure, things changed for the worse.

On October 2, 1943, the Germans passed the first racial law. All Jews in Athens were required to register within the next five days, the registration to take place in the synagogue. Those who did not register within that period were liable to death. Any Christians found aiding Jews were to be put into concentration camps. No Jew was to be allowed to change address without permission. No Jew was to be allowed on the street after 5 p.m. (General circulation is permitted in Athens up to 11 p.m.) As a result of these orders, 200 of the 8,000 Jews in Athens did register. 2,000 - 2,500 are believed to have joined the Antartes, and up to the present at least 500 have escaped to Smyrna.

The Greek police have proved helpful and sympathetic to the Jews, and the Germans have not insisted on enforcement of the new law; nevertheless, the Jews are very much afraid.

Sub-source came to the Consulate in Smyrna to report that David Tiano, "Commercial Attaché" at the Consulate in Salonica since 1920, was shot by the Germans. He had been arrested as a hostage, for no particular reason except that he was a Jew. Some three weeks later, while he was under lock and key, some sabotage occurred at the American Farm School. In reprisal, he and 15 others were shot. Somewhat later, and under circumstances not communicated, Emmanuel Cavassou, a secretary of the American Consulate at Salonica, was also shot.

Salonica

Of the 55,000 Jews formerly living in Salonica, there are now three left. These three have married Orthodox Greeks and embraced that faith.

Of all these Jews, informant (47 members of whose family were deported) knows of only one family that has been heard from. He believes the Germans were attempting a systematic extermination and therefore that some of the stories current about mass killings are undoubtedly true. As reason for believing that extermination was behind the deportation of the Jews from Salonica, he says that among those included were war victims, blind and maimed, some even legless, 150 from the insane asylum, 70 persons over 90, all the orphans and all criminals from the jails.

Escaping

Informant complains that getting people out of Greece has now become a racket. Caiques have been rented, or boats sold for high prices, and when a prospective evacuee arrives at the rendezvous, he waits indefinitely for a boat that never comes.

Informant believes captains of British caiques employ agents who tell the customers that they know a captain, etc., etc., and for a certain sum they can arrange to get the customer out. Informant thinks the captain certainly gets a cut of this money. Baggage is often taken on ahead, or it is said that it will follow by mule or other transportation. Not infrequently, owner never sees his property again. It is believed that this is not accidental.

Informant is by no means the first to complain, but he is the most lucid. . .

Report No. 19670
28 March 1944

SUBJECT: Military Information; Arrest of Jews.

Source: Reliable

1. The Germans have evacuated Egoumenitsa (R.53) and are reported, but not confirmed, also to have left Corfu.

2. A large German column moved on 27 March from Agrinion (X.43) to Yannina.

3. It is reported that heavy material is being moved from the Epirus area toward Salonica.

4. Zervas Antartes now occupy Parga (R.51)

5. Jews in Arta (X. 09), Prevesa (W.87) and Yannina (S.04) have been arrested and sent to Metsovon (S.35).

CONFIDENTIAL

Report No. 20097
March 26, 1944

SUBJECT: SS Activities in Athens

Source: Believed Reliable

1. The SS have begun mass arrests of Jews in Athens.

NOTES

1. The period and articles on the Jews, 1941-1944, has been recorded in J. O. Iatrides ed., *Greece in the 1940s: A Bibliographic Companion*, bibliographies by Hagen Fleischer and Steven Bowman, University Press of New England, Hanover and London, 1981. Other or more recent articles of interest include J. Ben "Jewish Leadership in Greece During the Holocaust", in *Patterns of the Jewish Leadership in Nazi Europe*, Yad Vashem, Jerusalem, 1977: R. Dalven, "The Holocaust in Janina" in *Journal of Modern Greek Studies*, Vol. 2 no. 1, May 1984; A. Kitroeff, "Greek Wartime Attitudes Towards the Jews in Athens", *Forum* 60, Summer 1987.

2. G. Th. Mavrogordatos, *Stillborn Republic: Social Coalitions and Party Strategies in Greece, 1922-1936*, University of California Press, Berkeley and Los Angeles, 1983.

3. S. E. Sevillas, *Athens-Auschwitz*, Lycabettus Press, Athens, 1983, edited and introduced by Nikos Stavroulakis.

4. Kitroeff, *op cit*. The most active resistance organization in this respect was EAM.

5. M. Vaphiades, *Apomnimonevmata*, Vol. II, Nea Sinora, Athens, 1985.

6. Ben, *op. cit.*; M. Molho and J. Nehama, *In Memoriam*, Jewish Community of Thessaloniki, Thessaloniki, 1976.

7. A more detailed resumé can be found in J. L. Hondros, *Occupation and Resistance: The Greek Agony 1941-44*, Pella, New York, 1983.

8. H. J. Hoppe, "Germany, Bulgaria, Greece: Their Relations and Bulgarian Policy in Occupied Greece" in *Journal of the Hellenic Diaspora*, Vol. XI, No 3, Fall 1984.

PUBLICATIONS CATALOGUE

Information is given below on ELIAMEP's (Hellenic Foundation for European and Foreign Policy) publications in the language in which each publication has been written.

Publications marked with an asterisc (*) are out of stock.

Επετηρίδες
Yearbooks

- ❏ YEARBOOK 1988 [Sp. issue: Greek Foreign Policy]

- ❏ The Southeast European YEARBOOK 1989 *

- ❏ The Southeast European YEARBOOK 1990 *

- ❏ The Southeast European YEARBOOK 1991

- ❏ The Southeast European YEARBOOK 1992

- ❏ The Southeast European YEARBOOK 1993

- ❏ The Southeast European YEARBOOK 1994-1995

- ❏ Επετηρίδα Αμυντικής και Εξωτερικής Πολιτικής '92:
  Η Ελλάδα και ο Κόσμος 1990-1991

- ❏ Επετηρίδα Αμυντικής και Εξωτερικής Πολιτικής '93:
  Η Ελλάδα και ο Κόσμος 1992

- ❏ Επετηρίδα Αμυντικής και Εξωτερικής Πολιτικής '94:
  Η Ελλάδα και ο Κόσμος 1993-1994

- ❏ Επετηρίδα Αμυντικής και Εξωτερικής Πολιτικής '95:
  Η Ελλάδα και ο Κόσμος 1994-1995

Ευρωπαϊκές και Διεθνείς Οικονομικές Μελέτες
European and International Economic Studies

- ❏ Problems of Intergrating the Soviet Economy
  A. Agabegyan, N. Petrakov, O. Bogolov,
  I. Ivanov, I. Korolyov (1990) *

❑ Η Ελληνική Στρατηγική
για τη Δημιουργία μιας Νέας Ευρώπης
Παναγιώτης Ιωακειμίδης (1990) *

❑ Η Ενταξη της Κύπρου στις Ευρωπαϊκές Κοινότητες
Πάνος Καζάκος (1990) *

❑ Special Report:
"The End of Central Planning? Socialist Economies
in Transition: The Cases of Czechoslovakia, Hungary, China
and the Soviet Union" (1990)
(Jointly with the Institute for East-West Security Studies)

❑ Prospects of the Greek Economy
Robert Mc Donald (1990) *

❑ Integration of the Greek Economy into the World Economy
and Balkan Economic Cooperation
Sotiris Wallden (1990) *

❑ Managing the Transition: Intergrating the Reforming
Socialist Countries into the World Economy
A Japanese View
Hiroaki Fujii *

❑ Die Integrationspolitischen Initiativen der
80er Jahre und die Griechische Europa Politik
Panos Kazakos (1992)

ΜΕΛΕΤΕΣ ΑΜΥΝΤΙΚΗΣ ΚΑΙ ΕΞΩΤΕΡΙΚΗΣ ΠΟΛΙΤΙΚΗΣ
DEFENSE AND FOREIGN POLICY STUDIES

❑ The Significance of Arms Control and
Disarmament in Europe
Theodore Couloumbis *

❑ Interdependence and East-European
Perceptions of Security: The Case of Bulgaria
Atanas Gotsev *

❑ Changes in Europe and their Implications for the Balkans:
A Romanian Prespective
Ioan M. Pascu *

❑ An Industry Without Frontiers: An Economic and Political
Analysis of European Defense Industrial Cooperation
Thomas S. Souleles (1990) *

❑ Η Ελλάδα-Τουρκία-Κύπρος,
Στρατιωτικά Στοιχεία και Αριθμοί 1990 - 1991
Αρ. Αριστοτέλους (1991) *
('Εκδοση από κοινού με το Κυπριακό Κέντρο Μελετών)

❑ Οι Διαπραγματεύσεις CFE και η Ελλάδα
Θ. Κουλουμπής, Γ. Βαληνάκης (Επιμ.) (1992)

❑ The "Macedonian Question"
an Historical and Diplomatic Review
Emmanuel Spyridakis (1991) *

❑ Τα Ηνωμένα Εθνη στην Υπηρεσία της Ειρήνης
Γεώργιος Κωστάκος (1992)*

❑ Η Αμυντική Πολιτική και Στρατιωτική Ισχύς της Τουρκίας:
Η Πρόκληση για την Ελληνική Ασφάλεια
Θάνος Ντόκος - Νίκος Πρωτονοτάριος (1993)*

❑ Boutros Boutros-Ghali's First Year at the Helm of the U. N.
Georgios Kostakos (1993) *

❑ Η Στρατιωτική Πλευρά της Κοινής Δράσεως
των Διαπλεκομένων Οργανισμών
Α. Δημητρακόπουλος (1993)

❑ Non-Proliferation and the Greek Foreign Policy
T. Dokos (1994)

❑ Προτεραιότητες Ασφάλειας της Ελλάδος
Α. Δημητρακόπουλος (1994)

❑ Greece and the New Europe
Y. Valinakis (1994)

❑ Προβλήματα που Δημιουργεί η Μη-μετατρεψιμότητα του
Ρουβλίου στις Δυτικές Επενδύσεις στη Ρωσία
και Τρόποι Αντιμετώπισης
Χ. Βλαχούτσικος (1994)

❑ Οι Οργανισμοί Ευρωπαϊκής Ασφάλειας
στο Νέο Περιβάλλον
Α. Δημητρακόπουλος (1994)

❑ Relations between Bulgaria and Greece
as Seen by their Political Elites
V. Todorov (1994)

❑ Το Νέο Στρατιωτικό Δόγμα της Ρωσικής Ομοσπονδίας
Α. Δημητρακόπουλος (1994)

❑ La Bilan du "Système de Barcelone"pour la Protection
de la Mer Méditerrranée Contre la Pollution
E. Doussis (1994)

❑ Modest Reforms and Practical Innovations
A Strategy for the Revision of the Maastricht Treaty
Panos Kazakos (1995)

Ειδικές Μελέτες και Μονογραφίες
Occasional Papers And Monographs

❑ Η Εμμεση Στρατηγική στην Ανατολική
Μεσόγειο και η Ελλάδα
Ν. Λαζαρίδης *

❑ Soviet Relations with Greece and Turkey
R. Eaton *

❑ The Impact of the Macedonian
Question on Civil Conflict in Greece, 1943-49
Evangelos Kofos (1989)

❑ U. S. Bases in the Mediterranean:
The Cases of Greece and Spain
T. Veremis - Y. Valinakis (1989) *

❑ Modern Greece: Nationalism and Nationality
Edited by M.Blinkhorn and T. Veremis (1990)
(Jointly with SAGE)

❑ Ισλάμ και Κράτος
Π. Γ. Βατικιώτης (1992)

❑ Η Ελληνοτουρκική Διαφορά για την Υφαλοκρηπίδα
του Αιγαίου Εναλλακτικές λύσεις και Προτάσεις
Χαριτίνη Δίπλα (1992)

❑ The Metaxas Dictatorship 1936 - 1940
Edited by Robin Higham and Thanos Veremis (1993)
(Jointly with the Speros Basil Vryonis Center
for the Study of Hellenism)

❑ The Power of the Vote: Lessons from Modern Greece
Dr. Kevin Featherstone (1995)

❑ Greece's Balkan Entanglement
Thanos Veremis (1995) / (Jointly with YALCO)

❑ Ελληνοτουρκικές σχέσεις (1986) *

❑ Από τη Λωζάννη [1923] ως το Παρίσι [1947] –
Η ισχύς και το κύρος των συνθηκών (1987)

❑ Διασφάλιση της Ποσοτικής και Ποιοτικής Αναλογίας
7 προς 10 στη Χορήγηση της Αμερικάνικης Βοήθειας
προς την Ελλάδα

❑ Ο Πόλεμος Ιράν - Ιράκ και οι Επιπτώσεις τυυ
στην Ελλάδα και την Τουρκία (1988)

❑ Προβλήματα Εναέριου Χώρου (1989)

❑ Κυπριακή Αμυνα - Μέρος Α' (1989) *

❑ Η Σημερινή Γιουγκοσλαβία (1990) *

❑ Introduction to Japanese Studies
G. Kostakos - G. Chronopoulos (eds) (1992)

❑ Arms Control and Security in the Middle East
and the CIS Republics
Th. Couloumbis - Th. Dokos (eds) (1995)

Από Άλλους Εκδότες
Jointly with other Publishers

The following titles have been published jointly with other publishers
and can be purchased from them exclusively:

❑ Ελλάδα - Τουρκία:
Αρθογραφικός Δείκτης 1979 – 1985
Θ.Βερέμης - Γ. Τσιτσόπουλος (επιμ.) (1987)
Εκδόσεις Παπαζήση

❑ Εγχειρίδιο Αφοπλισμού (ελλ. μετάφραση)
Andrew Wilson (1988)
Εκδόσεις Οδυσσέας

❑ Οι Ελληνοτουρκικές Σχέσεις 1923-1987
Α. Αλεξανδρής, Θ. Βερέμης, Π. Καζάκος,
Β. Κουφουδάκης, Χ. Ροζάκης, Γ. Τσιτσόπουλος (1991)
Εκδόσεις Παπαζήση

❑ Το Καθεστώς των Νησιών του Αιγαίου
Huseyin Pazarci - Κων/νος Οικονομίδης   (1989)
Εκδόσεις Γνώση

❑ Ελλάδα - Τουρκία: Αρθρογραφικός Δείκτης
Αμυντικής και Εξωτερικής Πολιτικής 1986 - 1989
Αλέξανδρος Αργυρόπουλος (επιμ.) (1990)
Εκδόσεις Παπαζήση

❑ Η Αμυντική Πολιτική των Βαλκανικών Κρατών
Γ. Βαληνάκης, Θ. Βερέμης, Κ. Ιορδανίδης,
Π. Κίτσος, Γ. Μούρτος, Γ. Χαρβαλιάς (1991)
Εκδόσεις Παπαζήση

❑ Αμυνα και Κοινή Γνώμη στην Κύπρο:
Ο Ρόλος της Ελλάδας και η Στρατηγική της Αποτροπής
Αρίστος Αριστοτέλους (1992)
Κυπριακό Κέντρο Σρατηγικών Μελετών

❑ Σημεία Τριβής στις Ελληνο-Τουρκικές Σχέσεις
Α. Γιόκαρης, Χ. Δίπλα, Α. Δημητρακόπουλος
Εκδόσεις Ι. Σιδέρης (1994)

❑ Η Στρατιωτική Ισχύς της Τουρκίας:
Η Πρόκληση για την Ελληνική Ασφάλεια
Θ. Ντόκος, Ν. Πρωτονοτάριος (1994)
Εκδόσεις Κ. Τουρίκη

❑ Το Χρονικό του Ζητήματος των Σκοπίων
Γ. Βαληνάκης, Σ. Ντάλης (επιμ.) (1994)
Εκδόσεις Ι. Σιδέρης

❑ Ελληνική Εξωτερική Πολιτική:
Προοπτικές και Προβληματισμοί
Θ. Βερέμης - Θ. Κουλουμπής (1994)
Εκδόσεις Ι. Σιδέρης

❑ Σκέψεις και Προβληματισμοί
για την Ελληνική Εξωτερική Πολιτική
Βύρων Θεοδωρόπουλος, Ευστάθιος Λαγάκος,
Γεώργιος Παπούλιας, Ιωάννης Τζούνης (1995)
Εκδόσεις Ι. Σιδέρης